Ming China, 1368–1644

CRITICAL ISSUES IN HISTORY

World and International History

The Vikings: Wolves of War
  by Martin Arnold
Magic and Superstition in Europe: A Concise History from Antiquity to the Present
  by Michael D. Bailey
War and Genocide: A Concise History of the Holocaust, Second Edition
  by Doris L. Bergen
Peter the Great
  by Paul Bushkovitch
A Concise History of Hong Kong
  by John M. Carroll
Ming China, 1368–1644: A Concise History of a Resilient Empire
  by John Dardess
A History of Medieval Heresy and Inquisition
  by Jennifer Kolpacoff Deane
Remaking Italy in the Twentieth Century
  by Roy Palmer Domenico
A Concise History of Euthanasia: Life, Death, God, and Medicine
  by Ian Dowbiggin
The Work of France: Labor and Culture in Early Modern Times, 1350–1800
  by James R. Farr
The Idea of Capitalism before the Industrial Revolution
  by Richard Grassby
The New Concise History of the Crusades
  by Thomas F. Madden
The Great Encounter of China and the West, 1500–1800, Third Edition
  by D. E. Mungello
A Concise History of the French Revolution
  By Sylvia Neely
The British Imperial Century, 1815–1914: A World History Perspective
  by Timothy H. Parsons
The Norman Conquest: England after William the Conqueror
  By Hugh M. Thomas
Europe's Reformations, 1450–1650: Doctrine, Politics, and Community, Second Edition
  by James D. Tracy

American History

The Unfinished Struggle: Turning Points in American Labor History, 1877–Present
  by Steven Babson
Conceived in Liberty: The Struggle to Define the New Republic, 1789–1793
  by Lance Banning
American Evangelicals: A Contemporary History of a Mainstream Religious Movement
  by Barry Hankins
The Evolutionists: American Thinkers Confront Charles Darwin, 1860–1920
  by J. David Hoeveler
The Conservative Century: From Reaction to Revolution
  by Gregory L. Schneider
America's Great War: World War I and the American Experience
  by Robert H. Zieger

Ming China, 1368–1644

A Concise History of a Resilient Empire

John W. Dardess

ROWMAN & LITTLEFIELD PUBLISHERS, INC.
Lanham • Boulder • New York • Toronto • Plymouth, UK

Published by Rowman & Littlefield Publishers, Inc.
A wholly owned subsidiary of The Rowman & Littlefield Publishing Group, Inc.
4501 Forbes Boulevard, Suite 200, Lanham, Maryland 20706
http://www.rowmanlittlefield.com

Estover Road, Plymouth PL6 7PY, United Kingdom

British Library Cataloguing in Publication Information Available

Library of Congress Cataloging-in-Publication Data

Dardess, John W., 1937–
    Ming China, 1368-1644 : a concise history of a resilient empire / John W. Dardess.
        p. cm. — (Critical issues in history. World and international history)
    Includes bibliographical references and index.
    ISBN 978-1-4422-0490-4 (cloth : alk. paper) — ISBN 978-1-4422-0491-1 (pbk. :
alk. paper) — ISBN 978-1-4422-0492-8 (electronic)
    1. China—History—Ming dynasty, 1368–1644. I. Title.
    DS753.D37 2011
    951'.026—dc22

                                                                            2011014079

♾™ The paper used in this publication meets the minimum requirements of
American National Standard for Information Sciences—Permanence of Paper
for Printed Library Materials, ANSI/NISO Z39.48-1992.

Printed in the United States of America

Contents

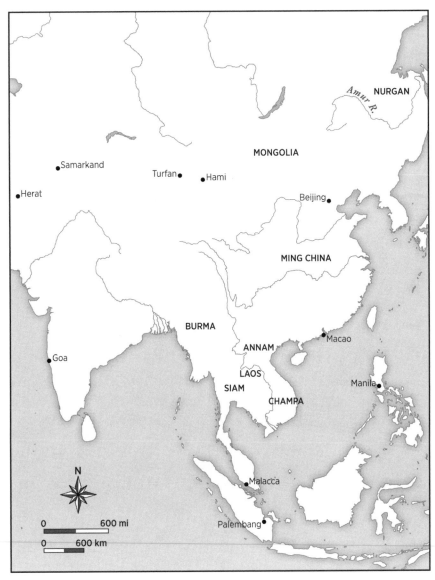

Map 1. Ming China in Asian context

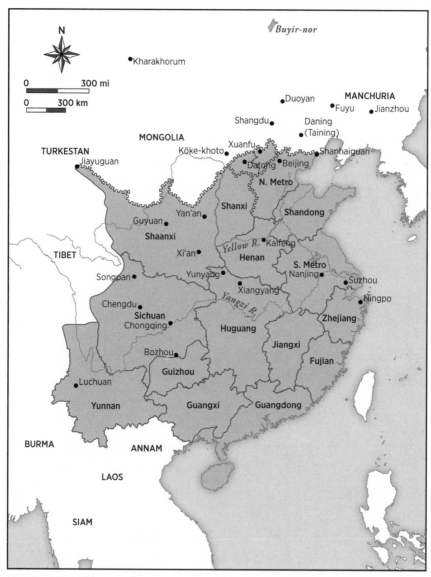

Map 2. Ming China provinces

Map 3. Modern provinces, Ming localities

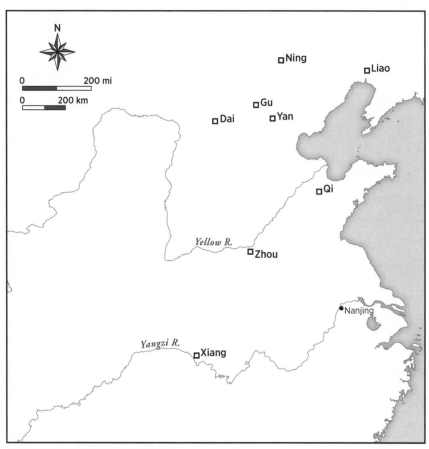

Map 4. Ming princedoms in 1398

~

The Ming Emperors:
Names and Dates

	Era Name	Dates	Personal Name	Posthumous Name
1	Hongwu	1368–1398	Zhu Yuanzhang	Taizu
2	Jianwen	1399–1402	Zhu Yunwen	Huidi
3	Yongle	1403–1424	Zhu Di	Chengzu
4	Hongxi	1425	Zhu Gaozhi	Renzong
5	Xuande	1426–1435	Zhu Zhanji	Xuanzong
6	Zhengtong	1436–1449	Zhu Qizhen	Yingzong
7	Jingtai	1450–1456	Zhu Qiyu	Jingdi
	Tianshun	1457–1464	Zhu Qizhen (again)	Yingzong
8	Chenghua	1465–1487	Zhu Jianshen	Xianzong
9	Hongzhi	1488–1505	Zhu Youtang	Xiaozong
10	Zhengde	1506–1521	Zhu Houzhao	Wuzong
11	Jiajing	1522–1566	Zhu Houcong	Shizong
12	Longqing	1567–1572	Zhu Zaihou	Muzong
13	Wanli	1573–1620	Zhu Yijun	Shenzong
14	Taichang	1620	Zhu Changluo	Guangzong
15	Tianqi	1621–1627	Zhu Youjiao	Xizong
16	Chongzhen	1628–1644	Zhu Youjian	Zhuangliedi

~

Preface

How does a person such as myself come to write a book such as the one now laid before the reader? I found, as I pondered the question, that this book has the particular subject matter and approach that it has for objective reasons to be sure, but also for reasons that are autobiographical.

I came upon China in 1959. That was long after an early childhood preoccupation with Adolf Hitler and the Third Reich (my father, a surgeon with Patton's Fourth Armored Division in World War II, was a hero to me). Hitler etched on my seven- and eight-year-old mind a deep impression of the evil impact of personality on history. After Hitler's demise, Stalin replaced him in my imagination. In March 1953 as a boy delivering newspapers, grim headlines announcing the tyrant's death struck me forcibly with both cheer and foreboding. In time, Stalin's departure opened space in my consciousness for Chairman Mao, but Mao lived in a world too remote for my comprehension, while the U.S.S.R. remained very much a threat. I took up the Russian language and history in college and only later had an opportunity, courtesy of the U.S. Army, to begin Chinese at the then Army Language School in Monterey, California. That was in 1959, and I have been involved with China ever since. A fascination with large political and military systems, in the charge of maniacal dictators, thankfully distant, that had such an impact upon me so early in my life has never completely faded. Childhood impressions are among the strongest impressions one has.

I came upon Ming China in the early 1960s at Columbia University. The Ming dynasty at the time was pioneering territory, a big blank in our knowledge of China's past. An arguably maniacal dictator founded it, namely Zhu Yuanzhang, or Ming Taizu, to use his posthumous name. Like Hitler and Stalin, Taizu rose to despotic power from humble origins and set in motion harsh and bloody plans to remake the world. So the Ming appealed to me. Wm. Theodore de Bary, with his interest in the thinker Huang Zongxi (1610–1695), had already launched what would turn out to be an outstandingly productive career as author and editor in Chinese intellectual history. He was also heavily involved in securing funding for the writing of the *Dictionary of Ming Biography*, which was based at Columbia, under the editorship of L. Carrington Goodrich and Chaoying Fang. A Ming seminar was organized in conjunction with it. Under the guidance of Fang and his wife, Lien-che Tu Fang, I wrote several biographies for the *DMB*, thanks to summer support President Lyndon B. Johnson's Great Society poverty funds provided. Indeed, I owe my career to the generous support, financial and otherwise, of the United States government. Perhaps that experience has led me, notwithstanding the autocrat who founded it, to a too positive view of Ming government, with its stipends for local Confucian students.

During my academic career at the University of Kansas, I wrote about Ming history chronologically, feeling my way through a landscape of whose basic features I was at the outset either ignorant or but vaguely grasped. First I wrote a book on the collapse of the preceding Yuan dynasty. Then a book on the Ming founding. Then a spin through the long middle years, through the perspective of local history. Then a book on late Ming. And now this.

Here I have chosen five approaches to Ming affairs, and arranged them in a cascade that begins with the outer edges of the Ming realm, then proceeds inward, and from the top down, from the emperors, to the officials, then to the literati, and finally to the outlaws and rebels who in conjunction with Manchu invaders from outside destroyed the whole system. I chose these five because they make sense to me. Another person with a personal background different from mine would probably have taken up themes different from these. But as I read the Ming situation, I find that the overriding concern of most people in the upper social echelons was to preserve it and sustain it by all available means. The perennial sources of existential threat lay along the thousands of miles of frontier, where lived turbulent ethnic entities of all sorts, and inside the realm as well, at the social frontier where some among the great masses of deprived and unlettered young Chinese males (and some females) periodically turned outlaw. Emperors and officials struggled to formulate policies to deal with these matters. So did literati out of office. The literati occupied an exceedingly complex middle position somewhere in between government and society. It was to them, acting in conjunction with outlaws and rebels, that the Ming dynasty owed its origins. Overwhelmingly, it is through them and all that they chose to write about that we know as much as we do about the Ming and its leading concerns. That, in a nutshell, is where this little book stands. I liked writing it and learned quite a bit doing it. And I hope that the reader enjoys it.

Despite all that I and many others have published over the years, so large is the available record that much about Ming China remains dimly understood, or positively misunderstood, or yet lies unexplored.

It is a pleasure to express my thanks to several people for their help and support: Vickie Fu Doll, Pam LeRow, Sarah Schneewind, Morris Rossabi, editors Susan McEachern, Alden Perkins, and Carrie Broadwell-Tkach, and an anonymous outside reader.

CHAPTER ONE

~

Frontiers

The Ming was durable. From its formal founding in 1368, to the Qing seizure of its capital, Beijing, in 1644, the regime successfully faced down all kinds of pressures and challenges, despite its many shortcomings. Its 276 years of existence are comparable in duration to the whole history of the United States from its foundation in 1776 to the time of this writing—234 years. Foreign relations, together with frontier management, were two of its primary responsibilities.

The Ming emerged in the wake of an experience of too much foreign interference—the Mongol Yuan dynasty. For a while, in the thirteenth century, China was no more than a part of a Mongolia-based empire that spanned much of the Eurasian continent. As of the time of its fourteenth-century creation, the Ming founders' strategy was strictly China-based. They limited the direct sway of its apparatus of governance to that part of the East Asian landmass that was settled, or was capable of being settled, by speakers of Chinese; people who, if educated, wrote in Chinese and who followed a repertoire of familial, social, and other customs that were identifiably and acceptably Chinese. Among the earliest acts of the founder was to notify the rulers of all other known socio-political entities that were geographically within reach that the Ming dynasty now controlled China, that it would expect periodic tribute embassies from foreign states, and would in return grant legitimacy and also a measure of protection to foreign rulers and their families, recognizing formally each orderly succession as it occurred. The founder's *Ancestral Instructions* enjoined his own successors to follow this plan. He also got up a curious list of foreign countries that China must never invade: Korea, Japan, the Ryukyus, Annam, Cambodia, Champa, Samudra (in Sumatra), the Western Ocean country (whatever that meant), Java, Pahang (on the Malay peninsula), Pajajaran (in Java), Srivijaya, Brunei. Although the Yongle emperor (r. 1402–1424) ignored this injunction, it was, generally speaking, respected for most of the Ming period. However, the founder did not include the countries or regions of Burma, Tibet, Eastern Turkestan (nowadays Xinjiang), Mongolia, or Manchuria. These unexplained but apparently deliberate omissions gave his successors wide latitude for aggressive settlement and military activity beyond the sphere of Chinese East Asia.[1]

Ming territory was about the size of modern France eight times over. It had the shape of a great irregular circle with eccentric lobes: one lobe in the southwest toward Laos and Burma, a second pushing into the Gansu corridor in the direction of the greater Middle East, and a third pressing into the Liaodong peninsula and southern Manchuria. The circumference of this circle, including the long seacoast, is hard to calculate, but it easily exceeds 7,000 miles altogether. Nearly every mile of that perimeter was susceptible to turmoil and violence. Much of it was contested.

Official Ming circles regularly used derogatory names to designate non-Chinese populations along the frontiers. The name "Lu" had raiders and robbers in mind and was invariably used with specific reference to the Mongol inhabitants of the northern steppes. The name "Wo," meaning "dwarf," referred both to Japan and to the partly Japanese pirates who raided the China coast especially in the sixteenth century. "Dog" signifiers regularly graced the written characters in use for many of the non-Chinese peoples in the southwest: the Lolo, the Zhuang, the Yao, and so on. Slightly less invidious were the names "Fan" (for Tibetan and similar groups to the west) and "Yi," for such as the Jurchens and other speakers of Tungusic languages in Manchuria, as well as for Europeans: the Dutch, for instance, were officially either "Red-haired Yi" or "Red-haired Fan."

The polite term *guo*, used by Ming founder Taizu for those entities he forbade his successors to attack, had in mind fairly large and fairly well-ordered hereditary monarchies that bent to conform their conduct of relations with China to the highly restrictive rules imposed by China. Indeed, the term *guo* applied to China itself—regularly "Zhongguo," the "central *guo*." At no time, however, did the label ever apply to any of the people of Mongolia. Only Altan Khan came close, when he personally was, with some deep reluctance, accorded the inheritable title "king" (*wang*) in 1570. But his people, mainly Tümed Mongols, never became a *guo*. Nor did Burma ever gain acceptance as a *guo*.

But not being styled a *guo* usually did not mean that Ming China refused somehow to absorb that entity into its framework of foreign relations. An entire system, applying principally to small or haphazardly organized ethnic groups along the southwestern and western frontiers, called the *tusi*, or "native administration areas," was patterned closely after the Ming international relations model—a bit along the lines of the U.S. federal government's recognition of some Native American tribes as in some ways sovereign entities. Though not styled *tusi*, a similar but more militarized system was imposed upon the non-Chinese inhabitants of the northwest and northeast frontier regions. The creation and institutionalization of all this was mostly accomplished during the reign of the Ming founder, 1368–1398, with additions, especially in the northeast, during the reign of Yongle, 1402–1424.

Ming China's land frontiers stretched in a great semicircle: from the subtropics bordering South and Southeast Asia, a lush landscape cut by sharp cliffs and deep ravines; then along the forested mountain edge of Tibet; to the desert, oasis, and grassland country of Qinghai, Gansu, and outer Shaanxi; then a stretch of some thousand miles along the line of the Great Wall, whose construction began in the late fifteenth century, and which China administered directly, and where nothing like a *tusi* system ever came into being; ending finally in the forested, sub-Arctic expanses of Manchuria out as far as the lower Amur river valley. The immensity taxes the imagination. And then there was the maritime frontier, completing the circle.

I propose to discuss Ming China's interactions with the larger world of its time by proceeding along the circle just described, beginning in the south, and ending in Manchuria. Then I'll continue with a look at Korea and Japan, followed by China's ocean frontier, and ending with the arrival by sea of the Portuguese, Dutch, and Spanish and the impact that they had upon the existing state of affairs. While each sector along the great circle makes a self-contained story of its own, it is well to remind ourselves that the Ming center regularly moved civil officials, generals, armies, and supplies from one distant theater to another over the 276 years of its existence.

We can start with north Vietnam, then known as Annam. It has been Vietnam's unhappy fate to be invaded from time to time by its giant neighbor to the north. Vietnam had from ancient times been administered as part of China.

It broke away as China itself broke up in the demise of the Tang dynasty in the tenth century. The Mongol Yuan made a punitive attack in 1287.

In 1788–1789, the Qianlong emperor did so again; and in 1979, China launched yet another punitive invasion. But none of those operations was as intensive as those the Ming conducted.

The late 1300s saw several Annamese incursions into the *tusi* chieftaincies on the Guangxi frontier. The Ming perceived these as a threat to regional security. But there was more. The ruling dynasty in Annam, the Tran, had peacefully agreed to submit to the Ming and enroll itself as a tributary state, with the privilege (or obligation) of sending periodic tribute and trade missions to the Ming capital, then Nanjing. In return, the Ming recognized the Tran as the legitimate and rightful rulers of the country. Then in 1400, a usurper violently deposed the Tran. A refugee of the royal family managed to escape to China, where he informed the Ming court of what had happened. After ascertaining the facts of the case, the warlike Yongle emperor (a usurper himself) decided to intervene on behalf of the Tran. He appointed a supreme commander, Zhang Fu, whose sister was one of Yongle's consorts. Zhang prepared an indictment listing twenty "crimes" committed by the post-Tran regime and threatening invasion unless the *status quo ante* were fully restored. When no satisfactory reply was forthcoming, the Ming made good on its threat. A land and sea operation involving some 215,000 troops descended upon Annam late in 1406. It met no stiff resistance. The Ming forces deposed the offending regime, whose backers melted into the countryside and, after a while, regrouped and began a guerrilla-style campaign against the Ming occupation.

It is immediately apparent from Zhang Fu's list that Annam was already administratively structured along Chinese lines. Its rulers also used written Chinese as their language for administrative purposes. Under the name Jiaozhi, Annam had many centuries before been part of the Qin, Han, and Tang empires. Zhang Fu therefore recommended the resuscitation of Jiaozhi, and its reannexation as a Ming province. The Yongle emperor agreed, and in July 1407, the deal was done. It was a mistake.

The Ming did try to "civilize" Annam, by opening Confucian schools, by discouraging ugly or shocking native customs, by rewarding collaborators, and by offering opportunities in China itself for the best and brightest. But there was a serious downside to the occupation. Ming palace eunuchs plundered the new province for its foreign trade and its pearls and precious metals. Ming Chinese officials dominated the upper levels of the provincial bureaucracy, leaving native administrators at ground level. Although the chief administrator, Huang Fu, did his best, there were limits on what he could do. The overall quality of the upper-level officials was poor, because no one who hoped to advance up the hierarchy in China wanted to go there, and therefore Jiaozhi became something of a dumping ground for examination failures from the nearby southern Chinese provinces. Many Annamese resented the annexation. Guerrilla resistance never died down. This forced the Ming to maintain an army of some 87,000 on-site and, in addition, forced Zhang Fu to carry out a number of expensive military reinterventions from outside.

In 1424, the Yongle emperor, whose attention had long since shifted away from Annam to the northern frontier and elsewhere, died. By 1427, the tide of the struggle turned. Ming forces suffered several serious defeats at the hands of the resistance leader, Le Loi, and began withdrawing back north. The futility of the annexation and the looming expense of yet another invasion prompted the Xuande emperor and his top advisors in the recently built Ming capital of Beijing to end the war and recognize Le Loi as the legitimate ruler of an independent and native-run Chinese-style dynasty. (Annam learned one lesson, and that was to turn upon its weaker southern neighbor Champa as the Ming had once turned upon it.)

For the next century, Ming relations with Annam remained fairly stable. Then the Le dynasty crumbled and was replaced in 1527 by a new regime, founded by Mac Dang-dung. Mac sought recognition and acceptance into Ming China's tribute system. China's top advisory board, the Grand Secretariat, was divided on the question of recognition (as they were also at the same time divided over the question of what to do about the Mongol-occupied Ordos region). One party, Grand Secretary Xia Yan's, wanted to invade and restore the Le. The other, led by Grand Secretary Yan Song, preferred a conciliatory approach. For the moment, the war party prevailed. In 1540, a Ming army of some 110,000 assembled on the Guangxi-Annam frontier, ready to march. The threat looked serious. Harsh terms were extended to Mac Dang-dung. He capitulated. Crawling barefoot before the seated Ming authority, he presented them copies of his tax registers and other documents, ceded some disputed border territory, and agreed to the nominal downgrading of his country from *guo* to native chieftaincy (*dutongshisi*).[2]

In the southwest, the front line of what was China interdigitated with settlements occupied from time immemorial by various Southeast Asian tribes and ethnicities. Here, Ming China exerted heavy pressure. The Mongols had done "China" a good turn when they destroyed the independent Dali kingdom in 1253, annexed its territory, created the province of Yunnan, and opened the place to Chinese immigration. The Ming founder, Taizu, in turn conquered Yunnan from its Mongol rulers in a massive and bloody invasion in 1382. He then ordered the roughly 250,000 ethnic Chinese troops who participated in that invasion to demobilize in situ and either bring in their wives or else marry local women. Altogether, Taizu moved some million Han (ethnic) Chinese into Yunnan and the southwest. Yunnan was vital at the time as Ming China's main source for copper, silver, gold, and other resources. The Ming implanted a military network of roads, post stations, forts, and garrisons (together administered by "pacification commissions"). These power nodes recruited natives as soldiers, maintained surveillance over the peoples of the southwest generally, and intervened with violence to suppress native raiders and settle native disputes.

This was the context for the operation of the Ming *tusi* system. It was international relations writ small. The Ming preferred this to large entities like the defunct Dali kingdom, which might pose a serious threat. The hereditary chiefs of the hundreds of *tusi* in the southwest were, pending good behavior, given titles that suggested their absorption into Ming bureaucracy, and were allowed to send tribute missions to the Ming capital every three years, or whenever it was necessary to confirm a succession. The chiefs, sometimes female, had full authority over their own tribespeople, but they were under the supervision of either the Ming Ministry of Personnel (if they were at least partly assimilated to China's ways) or the Ministry of War if they were not. Periodically provoked by Chinese settlers or official corruption or troubled by internal turmoil, these places would on occasion explode into violence and invariably suffer Ming military intervention in consequence. One would not go too far wrong in comparing the situation to contemporary Russia's violent relationships with Chechnya, Georgia, and other non-Russian entities in the Caucasus.

But Ming officialdom did not intend that the *tusi* should last forever. It waited for the arrival of yet more ethnic Chinese settlers to open underutilized land to irrigated agriculture and ply their business skills, until a "tipping point" was reached, and the tribal chiefdom was converted by official decree into prefectures and counties and fully annexed into Ming China's centralized bureaucratic system with centrally appointed Chinese magistrates. This process was called *gaitu guiliu*, or "turning native rule into regular administration." An early and wholesale example of the process was the creation in 1413 of Guizhou province, which encapsulated *tusi*-controlled territory as enclaves within China and no longer part of an external frontier at all.[3]

⌒

The southwestern *tusi* were regularly fought over by China, Burma, and upper Burma. Which of them would control the indigenous chieftaincies that lay between and among them?

Of these chieftaincies, the most powerful was the Shan kingdom of Luchuan, situated around what is now Tengchong in the southwestern Yunnan province. When the Ming invaded and annexed much of present-day Yunnan in the 1380s, Luchuan was not annexed, but retained semi-independence as a Ming pacification office under the hereditary local leadership of its *bwa*, or king. A Luchuan army of some 300,000 invaded Ming-controlled Yunnan in 1385, but the Ming viceroy Mu Ying and his firearm-equipped army defeated it. The Luchuan king, whose name is known in Chinese as Silunfa, then agreed to accept Ming suzerainty, and the Ming agreed to aid him against his rivals in Ava-Burma and elsewhere in the region.

Then, about a half-century later, a later Luchuan king, Sirenfa, tried to conquer various *tusi* along the Yunnan border that were under nominal Ming protection. Ming regional forces suffered a serious defeat in the course of trying to stop him. In these circumstances, the young Zhengtong emperor, guided by the war-minded palace eunuch Wang Zhen, authorized a massive military assault on Luchuan. In 1441 a war hawk and civil official, Minister of War Wang Ji (also a fine horseman and a lover of good food and music), was appointed supreme commander of 46,000 Yunnan troops plus 50,000 more men from neighboring provinces, and was directed to use them to crush Luchuan.

It must be noted in this connection that the decision to go to war was contested. Liu Qiu, a Hanlin official and imperial tutor, led the opposition to the Luchuan campaign. In a memorial to the throne, he argued that such a huge campaign was an overreaction to a small provocation, and a perilous drain on men and resources at a time when China faced a much more serious threat in the Oyirad Mongols led by Esen on the northern frontier. He urged the emperor simply to set up a military-agricultural colony near the Luchuan border and train local troops there. Rattled perhaps by Liu Qiu's logic, or suspecting a hidden agenda, Wang Zhen deeply resented his intrusion, and had Liu arrested and put in prison, where he was butchered and his corpse dismembered. Wang Ji's reply to this and similar arguments was that the Luchuan king had been generously treated by the Ming, that he had shown himself to be mendacious and treacherous, and that, unless suppressed with main force, the other chieftains in the region would cleave to him and pose a major threat to China's security along the entire southwestern edge of the realm. He went on to show that the operation was well planned, the logistics were in place, and that bilingual messengers were being sent to Luchuan with a warning for their leaders, giving them a chance to avoid war by returning everything they had looted, offering hostages, and capitulating to Ming authority.

Luchuan refused these terms, and so the campaign went off as originally planned. Wang Ji had overall command. Regular military officers directed the main columns. A palace eunuch, Cao Jixiang, had charge of firearms. Over the winter of 1441–1442, the Ming forces converged on King Sirenfa's central fortress, seized it, and burned it down, slaughtering many thousands in the process. Sirenfa and his family fled south to Ava-Burma. Wang Ji pursued them. The Ava king, Narapati, under threat, turned Sirenfa over to Ming custody, where he died, early in 1446.

The southwestern frontier remained volatile, even though Luchuan was removed from the map and its territory opened to Chinese immigration. Other chieftaincies still remained, however, and they posed difficulties. Chen Yongbin, governor of Yunnan province in the years 1593–1608, built a string of eight outposts designed to deter raiding, and entered into an agreement with the king of Siam to join him in an attack on Burma, which had been supporting the chieftaincies. The joint army burned the Burmese capital, Pegu, in 1600. (Things then quieted enough for the fugitive Southern Ming court to find refuge in Burma in 1659. Difficulties between China and Burma, however, continued into Qing and modern times.)[4]

Continuing north from Luchuan along the arc of Ming China's frontier, the next entity boasting a degree of size and power was the Miao chiefdom of Bozhou, which occupied a mountainous territory about the size of Switzerland lying some 300 miles north and east of what was once Luchuan. Under the rule of a hereditary leader known to us by his Chinese name, Yang Yinglong, the land of Bozhou broke apart in the 1590s in an internal war involving seven elite families, and this trouble may have prompted Yang to renege twice on his promise to contribute 5,000 troops to the ongoing Ming war against Hideyoshi and his Japanese army in Korea. It may also have led him to sustain himself by raiding and looting Ming territory in Guizhou and Sichuan provinces. In 1594, he inflicted a heavy defeat upon Ming forces in Sichuan. When the war in Korea ended in 1598, Ming China was ready to retaliate. A civil official, Li Hualong, was appointed governor of Sichuan and concurrently supreme military commander of the forces of the three provinces of Guizhou, Huguang, and Sichuan. Li estimated the enemy's strength as 140,000 or so men, organized and well motivated. He informed the war-minded Wanli emperor that at least that many Ming soldiers would be needed; and that while the gathering of that many men from the three provinces posed no great problem, supplying them did. It was going to require 1,500,000 silver taels that would have to be scraped together from a wide variety of sources all across the realm.

The funds were collected, the troops gathered, and after several months of hard fighting, eight separate Ming columns converged on Yang Yinglong's mountain stronghold. Li's leadership was inspired and effective. On July 15, the war was over. Yang Yinglong committed suicide, and his family was transported to Beijing for execution. Bozhou was abolished, its territory cut up into prefectures and counties and incorporated into China proper. Unused funds from the campaign were spent locally to help with rehabilitation and resettlement. Li gathered his many official memorials and dispatches relating to the campaign and published them. So did Guo Zizhang, governor of Guizhou, who helped with the campaign. One of Ming China's most renowned generals, Liu Ting, had a big part in the victory. It was one of the Ming army's prouder moments.[5]

Not many years after the conclusion of the Bozhou campaign, in 1619–1621, the largest of all the Ming frontier wars erupted in southwest China. It is often styled the "She-An" rebellion, in honor of the aristocratic Lolo warriors who headed it. Alternatively, it is called the Yongning rebellion, after the town (in later times Xuyong county) tucked into the southernmost extremity of Sichuan province, very close to Guizhou and Yunnan, that served as the seat of the native administration. The deeper origins of this war need not detain us, but the immediate cause lay thousands of miles away to the northeast in Manchuria, where Ming forces were engaged in war with a very difficult enemy, the people who would soon call themselves Manchus.

Expecting generous rewards, She Chongming voluntarily contributed 20,000 Lolo and other tribal warriors under his personal command to the Ming cause. This force set forth, accompanied by some 80,000 others: wives, children, servants and other hangers-on, plus animals. This veritable city on the move reached the Ming city of Chongqing, about a hundred miles to the northeast of Yongning, in October 1621. There the Ming governor of Sichuan province informed them that only actual fighters could be supported in a march across China. Everyone else had to go back home. The army rebelled on the spot. It seized Chongqing city and murdered the governor. Their ranks swelled with renegade Chinese to 100,000 or more. Chinese advisors signed on. She Chongming took the title King of Shu (Sichuan). The rebels took the town of Zunyi, recently the center of the defunct Bozhou regime. In Guizhou province, the Nasu Yi hereditary chief, An Bangyan, joined in with his fighters, and the Shu army snowballed into a huge force of some 300,000. The cities of Chengdu (capital of Sichuan) and Guiyang (capital of Guizhou) were laid under siege.

Neither city fell. A Ming civilian official, Zhu Xiyuan, supreme commander in Sichuan, eventually mobilized over half a million Chinese and as many non-Chinese troops, and organized supply lines involving some 450,000 men that stretched north and east for hundreds of miles into the Ming heartlands. After years of war, he prevailed. The cost of all this has been estimated as 35 million taels silver, plus two billion piculs of grain. And this in 1629, when time was running out for the Ming dynasty. The further reorganization of southwest China would have to wait until Qing times.[6]

From south to north, the outer (western) frontier of Sichuan province extended some seven hundred straight-line miles to a region where it met what was then still part of Shaanxi province, but is now the separate province of Gansu. Today's Sichuan extends several hundred miles further west to include a large slice of the Tibetan plateau, whereas in Ming times it feathered off at the base of that plateau, where non-Chinese *tusi* settlements were to be found in some number.

Generally speaking, the population along this Sichuan-to-Shaanxi frontier was "Tibetan," but it also included people, perhaps related, designated as Qiang and as Tangut, or Mi-nyag. In Ming times, there was a tendency for what may be called Tibetan civilization to drift eastward from Lhasa and regroup along the Ming frontier.

Ming China engaged this Tibetan world on three levels. First, there was a heavy demand in China for horses, mainly for military use, and so Ming government established a monopoly over Sichuan tea production and traded the tea for Tibetan horses at designated stations along the frontier, principally in Shaanxi. Second, Ming government was always interested in maintaining good relations with the various Tibetan Buddhist sects, inviting the monks to visit China, and permitting as many as a thousand of them at a time to live in designated temples in Beijing. Third, there lay along the frontier the hereditary settlements, or *tusi*, whose leaders had the same sort of relationship to Ming government as the leaders of the *tusi* to the south in Yunnan, Guizhou, or Guangxi. The Tibetan population was thinner, however, and the raiding and other violence their young men engaged in less menacing.

One of the larger Ming military operations involving Tibetans (or Qiang, or Mi-nyag) centered upon Songpan. A walled frontier town, Songpan lay about 150 miles north of the Sichuan provincial capital of Chengdu, in the scenic forested foothills of the Tibetan plateau. It housed a Ming guards commandery. The commandery's purpose was to control a much larger hinterland consisting of Qiang or perhaps Tibetan settlements. But the Tibetans, if that is who they were, had long enjoyed the protection of their high unapproachable mountain stockades. From these they conducted raids. Sometime early in the sixteenth century, a Chinese commander used incendiary arrows of his own invention to set their stockades and the felt clothing of their fighters ablaze and for a time stop their raiding. In the mid-sixteenth century, local raiders accepted protection from Altan Khan's Mongol regime in the Ordos. Local Ming commanders failed to stop the raiding because all they could think of was to mount large expeditionary armies, which the raiders could easily block in the rugged terrain. This was taking place at a time when the Sichuan population was growing restive owing to incessant and exploitative timber extraction by Ming government. It was warned that some awful disaster was in the making. But by 1588, Sichuan governor Xu Yuantai was able to describe in two long reports the bloody but patient destruction of much of the raiders' infrastructure of mountain redoubts, thanks in great part to the work of the Ming general in charge, Li Yingxiang, and his 50,000 troops.[7]

Proceeding north from Sichuan along the arc, the next component of the Ming frontier was the Gansu Corridor section of Shaanxi province, where the oblong tents of the Tibetans gave way to the round felt tents of the Mongols, and the forested mountains faded into Ming China's desert gateway to and from Turkestan and the Middle East. This was culturally a very mixed world, where Tibetan, Mongol, Chinese, and Turkic Muslim communities could be found living in fairly close proximity to one another. Ming armies conquered Gansu in the 1370s, and although the term *tusi* was never used in reference to the non-Chinese and their leaders out here, a very similar arrangement was involved when the Ming authorities organized the surrendered Mongol and other, mainly Turkic, inhabitants into Ming-style military units (*wei*). The nomenclature here was the same as that used for the regular Ming army, whose leadership positions were also hereditary. Here, 400 miles northeast of Songpan, lay the county of Guyuan, which gave its name to a frontier war that took place in the region in 1468 and 1469.

The causes of the rebellion are not clear. In any case, the leader of it was a "local Tatar" (Tuda) by the name of Man Si. Man Si was a huntsman and rich cattle baron and leading member of a tribe or group of Mongols who surrendered to Ming forces in the 1370s and were given hereditary positions in the Pingliang Guards (Pingliang was located some hundred miles northwest of the Shaanxi provincial capital of Xi'an). Man Si built himself a base much farther to the northwest, at a secure site called Shicheng ("Stone City"), high in the rugged mountains about another hundred miles northwest of Pingliang. He thus ensconced himself on the ill-defined western frontier of the Ming, and the Ming authorities in Beijing were concerned that he might make common cause with the Mongols to his northeast.

The Tuda were clearly not considered to be Chinese. "They are not our kind," wrote historian Gao Dai later on, in the sixteenth century, "and their minds are different." Even so, many of their leaders, including Man Si, bore Chinese names, and had long been much more tightly integrated into the hereditary Ming officer class than the *tusi* chiefs of the southwest. Indeed, one of the career Ming commanders, a Tuda Mongol of similar background to Man Si and who fought him on Ming behalf, was Mao Zhong or Mao Khara ("khara," meaning "black," was a common Mongol name; his dates are 1394–1468), who was elevated into the Ming military nobility as an earl. Some Chinese, escaping onerous labor services, fled west to Man Si, seeking his protection. This quasi-ethnic revolt against the Ming was put down only after a long siege, involving a very large force, of Man Si's mountain fortress. The fortress was completely razed. Man Si was captured, and in 1469 he was executed in Beijing.[8]

⌒

Ming China's westernmost point was Jiayuguan, in the desert and oasis country of the Gansu Corridor, where a small garrison was posted in 1372 and a fort built. Beyond Jiayuguan lay eastern Turkestan (nowadays Xinjiang province) where the Chaghatai khans of Central Asia held nominal sway. Beyond Jiayuguan, the closest city to China was Hami, some three hundred miles to the northwest. Two hundred miles west of Hami lay the city of Turfan. Ming China had some difficult relations with both.

A thousand five hundred miles west of Jiayuguan was Samarkand, Tamerlane's capital. Ming Taizu sent two embassies there, as part of his general program of informing foreign rulers of the Ming founding and strongly urging their acceptance of a tributary relationship to China. Neither embassy ever returned. Tamerlane was angered by the belittling tone of the Ming court's address to him. Ming government was not aware that he planned a massive military assault on their empire. He and his army of some 200,000 entered winter camp in Utrar, several hundred miles north of Samarkand. World history was spared a stunning clash of very large armies when Tamerlane died of illness in that camp in February 1405, and the whole operation was canceled.

The Yongle emperor had better luck than Taizu contacting Tamerlane's successors—his son Shahrukh in Herat and grandson Ulugh Beg in Samarkand. It was always possible for China's emperors to drop the tributary language and deal with foreign rulers as equals if need be, and Yongle did so here. Envoy Chen Cheng's famous first trip to Herat took a year and a half, from February 1414 to November 1415. He made another trip in 1416–1417. A third mission, led by eunuch Li Da, was sent in 1418–1419. Chen Cheng's final mission took place in 1420–1421. The various Central Asian rulers sent large return missions to China. Chen Cheng's reporting made it clear that Herat, for all its strangeness, was no barbarian stronghold, but a civilized place. It looked as though relations between China, Central Asia, and the greater Middle East might deepen and thicken with the passage of time, but that was not to be. Great political changes took place during the sixteenth century, as the Timurid Empire crumbled, and new nomad combinations (Kirghiz, Kazakh, Turkmen) emerged to raid the cities and towns, which were left to fend for themselves. Ming China chose to back away and not involve itself in the turmoil.

Although the oasis city of Hami was in Han, Tang, and Yuan times under military rule from China, it lay beyond the Ming founder's line of vision. The Yongle emperor, expansion-minded as he was in every direction of the compass, sought to bring it under Ming control; and while he refrained from trying to conquer it outright, he did establish a very satisfactory tributary relationship with its Uighur and Buddhist rulers. Frequent trade missions from Hami and points farther west brought much-needed horses plus a range of other goods to the border and on to the capital in Beijing. But sometime during the first half of the fifteenth century, the rulers and people of Hami, formerly Buddhist, converted to Islam. Competition then developed between Ming China and Turfan over Hami: would it continue to lie in China's orbit, or would it fall to Turfan, and so become the easternmost outpost of a Muslim regime whose main interests lay less with China than with the larger Muslim world to the west? Ming China tried but failed to hold Hami. By the early sixteenth century it gave up and let it go. The state-managed tea-horse trade with Central Asia declined and disappeared later in that same century.[9]

⌒

From Jiayuguan, the great arc of the Ming frontier bent generally northeast, and for some 1,500 miles fronted on the limitless grasslands of Mongolia, with its thin but formidable population of pastoral nomads. Yet over the whole span of Ming history, there is no doubt but that it was those Mongols who posed the most intractable problems for Ming governance. A glance at the huge document collection called the *Huang Ming jingshi wenbian*, published in 1639 (to be discussed a bit more later), shows a heavy skewing toward northern frontier issues: garrisoning; troop recruitment, training, and deployment; walls and fortifications; armaments; supply; horse procurement and management; border trade policy; tributary relations difficulties—plus all the problems of building, repairing, and modifying the huge logistics infrastructure necessary to the support of frontier defenses: Grand Canal upkeep; Yellow River conservancy; the salt and tea monopolies as crucial fiscal underpinnings.

In September 1368, the Mongol Yuan court evacuated Beijing (then called Dadu) and reestablished itself at its summer capital, Shangdu, about two hundred miles north in eastern Inner Mongolia. Some Chinese officials accompanied it. They and the Yuan court had some thought of reentering China and reestablishing the Yuan at some point in the near future. The Ming founder knew or guessed this, and acted to ensure that never happened. Several Ming military expeditions entered deep into Mongolia. A Ming attack of 1370 forced the Yuan court to retreat from Shangdu to Kharakhorum, nearly a thousand miles to the northwest. In 1388, a huge Ming expedition inflicted a massive defeat upon the Yuan at Buyir-nor in easternmost Mongolia. Captured were 150,000 animals, 77,000 Mongols male and female, 3,000 officials, plus the Yuan imperial harem and several princes. The ruler himself escaped but was soon murdered by his own people. The action brought the Ming some twenty years of peace and quiet on the northern frontier.

For some eighty years, the Ming dynasty's northern strategy was to prevent the rise of any unifying power in the steppes, which in turn seems to have required that Ming armies continue campaigning into the steppes in alliance with weaker Mongol groups in order to inflict damage on the stronger. This activity reached a peak during the Yongle emperor's reign, 1402–1424. It was the Mongol problem that drove him to move the capital from Nanjing to Beijing, near the northern frontier. Yongle led in person no fewer than five expeditions into the steppes, most of them in opposition to Arughtai, the strongest of the would-be unifiers. The first campaign in 1410 met with some success, as Arughtai was forced to agree to tributary subordination to China; but those that followed yielded indifferent results. Still the strategy held good until the traumatic turn of events occasioned by the Tumu incident of 1449, when an expedition under the command of the young Zhengtong emperor and his aggressive chief eunuch, Wang Zhen (who pressed to launch the 1441 Luchuan campaign, as noted above), was ambushed at the Tumu postal station, about one hundred miles northwest of Beijing and forty miles southeast of the frontier garrison town of Xuanfu. The eunuch was killed, and the emperor was captured and made hostage by Esen, the new unifier of the steppe tribes. Beijing was thrown into a panic. Then the top officials decided to depose the Zhengtong emperor in absentia, replace him with his younger brother, and thus rob him of any further value to Esen. Esen fumbled away his momentary advantage over China. But Ming China needed to devise some new frontier strategy.

It had a hard time doing so. The Tumu shock polarized Ming attitudes toward the Mongols for many years; fierce partisan debates featured militants, active appeasers, and passive defenders. What Esen wanted from China was access to China's goods by way of border markets and tributary embassies to Beijing. Failing that, he had to resort to the less satisfactory alternative of plundering raids into Ming territory. In the view of Beijing, however, trade was a privilege to be granted reluctantly and stintingly, but only if the other party showed good and submissive behavior. Beijing refused to negotiate with Esen. Until 1571, it refused to negotiate with any of his successors. So the Mongols raided, and the Ming, no longer in a position either fiscally or in terms of confidence and morale to launch any more punitive expeditions, turned to the only practicable choice that remained: to build up its defenses all along the northern frontier, from Jiayuguan at the westernmost extremity, 1,500 miles east to Shanhaiguan. Construction began on what Westerners came to know as the Great Wall at its extreme eastern end in the 1440s and in Shaanxi in the far west in the 1470s. A fifty-year gap followed, then construction began again in earnest. The job was never completed. Construction and reconstruction were still in progress when the Manchus took Beijing in 1644. The term "great wall" was not in use in Ming times. The term used was *jiu bian*, the "nine frontier garrisons," referring to the main garrison towns spotted along the frontier that together with the walls, the signal stations, the fighting towers, military farms, and other accoutrements made up the whole defensive system. The human and fiscal costs of building and maintaining all this were truly staggering.

The Ming defense lines, walls and all, were no more impermeable to Mongol raiders than the elaborate fencing of the Mexican border is these days a total barrier against drug runners and illegal migrants. Denied authorized access to China, the Mongols continually probed for weak spots. A favored staging area for raids was the cultivable north loop of the Yellow River as it bends around the Ordos desert. Here Altan Khan (1507–1582), leader of the Tümed Mongols, built settlements, including a capital city of sorts called Blue City (Köke khoto, nowadays Hohhot), welcomed in Chinese religious sectarians and other fugitives as settlers, and carried on a lively smuggling trade with Ming soldiers and others on the other side of the frontier. Meanwhile, he tried again and again to negotiate with the Ming court, which time and again rejected his overtures, whereupon deep plundering raids into China would follow. In 1550, he raided as far as the city walls of Beijing and got the court to agree to open border markets, but the Ming soon shut them down again.

For years, debate raged in Beijing about whether or not to punish Altan Khan and avenge China's honor by invading and annexing the Ordos region that served as his base of operations. The costs promised to be astronomical. Intense bureaucratic infighting over the issue peaked in the 1540s. The Jiajing emperor, earlier a backer of the annexationists, was persuaded in 1548 to turn against them. Their leaders, Chief Grand Secretary Xia Yan and Vice Minister of War and supreme commander on the Shanxi frontier Zeng Xian, were executed. Yan Song, Xia's enemy and successor as chief grand secretary, championed a wholly defensive stance. No agreement with Altan Khan could be negotiated until after the Jiajing emperor's death in 1566. Then it required the extraordinary political power of Chief Grand Secretary Zhang Juzheng at last to push through and enforce a peace agreement with Altan Khan in 1571.

The agreement granted Altan Khan the title Shunyi wang ("prince who conforms to righteousness") and gave his capital the new name of Guihua ("return to civilization"). Regular border markets and tributary trade were authorized. Altan became eager to associate his regime with the Yellow Hat (Gelukpa) sect of Tibetan Buddhism, and Beijing was happy to assist with that, by providing him with Tibetan lamas, holy scriptures, and translations of sacred texts from Tibetan into Mongolian. These arrangements benefited all sides and were popular with everyone who lived on either side of the northern frontier. But Zhang's bureaucratic opponents considered it a corrupt bargain and would have none of it. Altan Khan and Zhang Juzheng died in the same year, 1582. Zhang was posthumously condemned. The agreement gradually fell apart. Once again the top item in China's foreign policy succumbed to a politicized Confucian moralism.[10]

Continuing eastbound along the great arc of China's perimeter, one came upon a transition zone between the Mongolian steppes and the Manchurian forests, a mixed region sporting steppe, forest, and some agricultural possibilities that in Ming times was occupied by a curious agglomeration of people known as the Three Commanderies (of Duoyan, Fuyu, and Taining). They were also referred to as the Uriyangkhad. They were at least in part speakers of one or another Mongol dialect, and perhaps a Tungusic dialect as well. Semi-migratory, as were many groups and tribes in Manchuria proper, the Uriyangkhad were, when the commanderies were created by the Ming in 1389, located some four hundred miles northeast of the old Yuan summer capital of Shangdu. Squeezed between more powerful Mongol neighbors to the west and the Manchurian tribes on the east, the Uriyangkhad played a middleman's game, which led them to cooperate with China from time to time. Though they occasionally misbehaved, conducting raids on China or throwing support to Ming enemies, they remained through Ming times a fairly reliable ally against Mongol combinations to the west; and even when they weren't, Beijing usually kept open tributary and trade relationships with them anyway.[11]

From Uriyangkhad territory we continue going east. The vast region commonly known in the West as Manchuria fell gradually into the Ming orbit, beginning in 1371. In a series of actions ending in 1387, a massive Ming assault on the Yuan Mongol governor of Liaodong (as southern Manchuria was called) ended in his surrender. A sad column of 200,000 soldiers plus animals stretched in a long line as they plodded off to China proper. The surrendered troops were divided into small units, incorporated into the Ming army, and posted to various far-flung parts of the realm. This operation mirrored the conquest of Yunnan in 1382, except that Liaodong was not made into a province but instead became a militarized zone under the control of guards units, many of them consisting of people known as Jurchens. The whole was put under the supervision of Shandong province to the south.

The Yongle emperor (r.1402–1424), pushing outward to nearly every point of the compass, reached out beyond Liaodong into Nurgan, an enormous region along the lower Amur river. A Jurchen eunuch by the name of Isiha paralleled in his part of the world the activities of a Yunnan Muslim eunuch by the name of Zheng He and his voyages to Indonesia and points west, to be noted below. Isiha was put in charge of six expeditions into Nurgan. The first was launched in 1411 with twenty-five riverboats and a thousand men, mainly for demonstration effect. Isiha contacted some 178 tribes and gave hereditary military offices to their leaders along with trade opportunities and the privilege of periodic visits to the Ming capital. In 1413, in an effort to civilize the tribes, Isiha and his entourage built a Buddhist temple, the Yongningsi, in Nurgan territory in a spot well over a thousand miles northeast of Beijing, not far from where the Amur river empties into the Sea of Okhotsk. A stele in four languages (Chinese, Mongolian, Tibetan, and Jurchen) triumphantly explained to any who could read the Ming mission of peace and good order. However, the inoculation failed. The temple somehow got destroyed. The Ming rebuilt it in 1433, with a new inscribed stele. But it too was eventually abandoned. In line with Yongle's general policy of pulling back advanced outposts all along the western, northern, and eastern frontiers—an ironic counterpoint to his expansionism in other respects—the Ming soon withdrew and never again tried to return to Nurgan. Liaodong (southern Manchuria) stayed in the Ming orbit, however. Its tribes were at times troublesome, but no major threat developed there until the rise of Nurhaci and his Jianzhou Jurchens (later, Manchus) in the late sixteenth and early seventeenth centuries. Up until that time, the Ming meddled in the tribal situation, successfully prevented the tribes from forming menacing combinations, and so kept them capable of nothing beyond raiding. The Ming also successfully warded off Mongol and Korean intervention.[12]

South of Manchuria lay the Korean peninsula. Nowadays, China and North Korea confront one another directly along the Yalu and Tumen rivers. In Ming times this was not the case, as Ming control in Manchuria was never more than indirect. Early in Ming times, both China and Korea involved themselves with the Manchurian tribes, each trying to identify and defend friends, punish enemies, and achieve thereby some measure of frontier security. Thanks to its superior resources, the Ming prevailed, and Korea eventually withdrew.

Ming China regarded Korea as an ordered society, a *guo*, one that, while certainly foreign, had over the centuries absorbed much of China's civilization, including its Buddhism, Confucian ethics, and its written language. However, Korea was small, and the Ming imperial court often felt free to bully it, demanding from it eunuchs, concubines, horses, and various luxury goods.

It took some years for Korea to settle comfortably within the strict confines of the Ming tributary system. Until the Ming conquest of Mongol-controlled Manchuria in 1387, the Korean court could not give its full allegiance to the Ming. In 1388, as the Ming tightened its grip in Manchuria, a dispute arose over control of territory that the Korean court considered to be Korean. The Korean court launched a military campaign to reclaim it. The commander of the campaign, Yi Sŏng-gye, believed the operation ill-advised, turned his army around, marched on the capital, deposed the court, and in 1392 established his own dynasty, the Yi, which would last until the Japanese annexation of 1910. But the Ming court was suspicious of all this, and for various reasons refused to accept the Yi as genuine. Not until 1402 did the Yongle emperor, who had himself just usurped power in China, and in need of foreign recognition, grant full legitimacy to Yi-ruled Korea.

After 1402, Ming-Korea relations remained fairly stable. As was true elsewhere, Ming embassies to Korea grew fewer in the years that followed, while Korean pressure to expand trade and other opportunities in China grew heavier and heavier. Late in the sixteenth century, the Ming emperor Wanli made good on the moral obligation implicit in the tributary relationship, that China would try to defend a state whose legitimacy it recognized if it came under attack. In 1592, Japan invaded Korea. The Japanese dictator, Hideyoshi, had China's conquest ultimately in mind; and whether or not the Ming realized that, the Manchurian border was clearly under threat. The war-minded Wanli added border security to the moral dimension of the issue and made the decision to intervene on Korea's behalf. Suffice it here to say that China and Japan each mobilized hundreds of thousands of troops, that the war in the peninsula raged on and off for six years, until 1598, when Hideyoshi died, and the Japanese withdrew. In 1601, the Ming forces too returned home.

The war inflicted heavy damage on the peninsula. And very soon, on top of that, the Ming called upon Korean troops to help in its war against

Nurhaci and his Jurchens in Manchuria in 1619. From 1621 to 1629, a Ming general, Mao Wenlong, used Korean territory as a base from which to direct a series of raids and sorties against the Jurchens. Korea had to comply, at great cost to itself. The soon-to-be Manchus were convinced by Mao Wenlong's behavior that they would have to invade Korea and make it a vassal state. That they did, in 1636.[13]

⁓

From Manchuria, extending south, then bending gradually to the west, lay well over 2,500 miles of coastline, a maritime frontier. Beyond it, not far from Korea, lay the powerful island empire of Japan. Like Korea, Japan had religious, cultural, and commercial ties of long standing with China; and the founders of the Ming dynasty recognized it as a *guo* on a par with Korea, Annam, and Champa, and in 1368 invited the ruler of the country, whoever he might be, to enroll as a tributary in the Ming system. There at once developed some serious difficulties and misunderstandings, owing mainly to internal political turmoil in Japan. This irritated Taizu, the Ming founder. Ignoring his own written instructions to his successors, he threatened an invasion. In 1382, Prince Kanenaga of the Southern Court responded to the threat by questioning the very legitimacy of the Ming claim to world dominion. Not until Taizu died in 1398 did things ease and relations improve. As he did with others, Yongle reached out to Japan. The Ashikaga shogun Yoshimitsu reacted favorably, and from 1404 to 1549, nearly a century and a half, relations with the Ashikaga Shogunate were conducted on a tributary basis, with occasional snags and disputes, but on the whole satisfactorily for both sides.

The two sides agreed that their sizable mutual trade would come completely under political control; and that in return for trading privileges, the shogunate would help to suppress the endemic coastal piracy in which Japanese nationals were involved. But like the Mongols, Koreans, and everyone else, the Japanese constantly pressed to increase the size and frequency of their trade missions, while the Ming authorities, saddled with the heavy expense of operating the tribute system, and ideologically opposed to expanding trade, tried just as hard to keep things under tight restriction.

In 1549, the last Japanese mission departed Beijing for the voyage home via the port of Ningbo. The Ashikaga Shogunate, never in complete control of Japan, was deep in its decline phase, and the Ōuchi daimyo family, feudal lords who had lately dominated the China trade, fell apart in 1551.

All trading connections with Ming China, which had been growing, became privatized—as out-and-out smuggling and piracy.

The endemic piracy problem along the China coast surged in the mid-sixteenth century. Although the Japanese ports continued to serve as bases of operations, Japanese nationals at this time no longer had a major role as raiders. Chinese, led by maritime entrepreneurs such as Wang Zhi, took their place. Even so, it was convenient for officialdom to continue to label all coastal pirates as *wokou*, "dwarf (i.e., Japanese) bandits." This was because fighting foreigners led to higher rewards than fighting internal bandits, and because labeling piracy as a foreign phenomenon eased investigative pressures on coastal elites, especially in Fujian province, who were in fact heavily engaged in it. While the Ming court wavered between harsh methods and accommodative gestures toward the pirates, a combination of a defensive buildup along the coast (walls around cities and county seats, military bases, signal stations) and the deployment of a cohort of brilliant military tacticians (including especially Qi Jiguang, active along the Zhejiang and Fujian coasts from 1556 to 1567, when he was transferred to the northern frontier) gradually imposed a degree of security and order. Equally important was a major policy reversal emanating from Beijing with the enthronement of a new emperor—Longqing, early in 1567: the decision to ease the long-standing ban on maritime trade, legalizing what only smuggling and piracy had made possible previously.

Japan itself, torn by civil war, was not officially contacted until its would-be unifier Hideyoshi invaded Korea in 1592. After much debate, the Ming court sent a mission to Japan in 1596 with the aim of investing Hideyoshi as King of Japan and enrolling him as a Ming vassal. Apparently it was the demeaning tone of the Ming letter of investiture that most infuriated Hideyoshi (reacting to Ming verbiage as Tamerlane had two centuries before). Hideyoshi refused to accept the letter and renewed the stalemated war in the Korean peninsula.

There is no little irony in Japan's behavior after the Ming fell in 1644. Although no official relations between Japan and China existed, the Tokugawa Shogunate, founded in 1600, made strong moves in 1641 to limit the country's foreign contacts, much in line with the pattern the Ming had established and maintained through most of its history.[14]

As we proceed south along the coasts of Zhejiang and Fujian, we come at last to Guangdong province and the port city of Canton (Guangzhou), and thereby bring to a close our great circle tour of the Ming frontiers. Guang-dong had its troubles with pirates and bandits, but we shall not pause to detail the matter here. Instead, we will use this as a convenient point to take up an issue more relevant to the story of Ming China's place in the world: the Zheng He voyages of the early fifteenth century.

There are two affairs of Ming vintage that remain to this day as symbols of Chinese ethnic pride and identity: one is the Great Wall, which in Ming times was never singled out for its symbolism; and the other the seven voyages to the "South Seas" conducted by the Yunnanese Muslim eunuch Zheng He in the years 1405–1431, which in Ming times were controversial and were canceled and mostly forgotten after the return of the last one in 1433. But the voyages deserve mention nevertheless.

The ships used by Zheng He were not built in Canton. They were built at a dockyard in Nanjing. The first voyage consisted of 317 of these ships carrying 27,870 men to Calicut in south India, with intermediate stops at Champa, Malacca, Java, and other places. The men fought a successful battle against a Chinese pirate and his forces at Palembang (southern Sumatra), and brought back to China tributary envoys from some half-dozen kingdoms and sultanates to present their offerings to the Ming court. Later voyages reached as far as Mecca, Somalia, and Kenya. These were imperial exhibitions, however. They were not commercial ventures. Merchants of coastal China had no part or stake in them. The voyages were set in motion by the fiat of the Yongle emperor, and they were terminated, due mainly to their high cost, at the command of another emperor, Yongle's grandson, Xuande. Ironically, less than a century after the end of the Zheng He voyages, the tide reversed, and the Portuguese, eastbound and commerce-minded, pioneered the Western penetration of East Asian waters with their conquests of Goa in 1511 and Malacca (or Melaka, a Ming tributary no less) and their establishment there of royal governance, the Estado da India.

It is a mistake easily made to overstress from the Ming perspective the significance of the opening of maritime China to Western contact in the sixteenth and seventeenth centuries. The attention of Ming officialdom was mainly focused on the northern frontiers, and secondarily on the Japan-based sea raiders. Portugal, Spain, and the Netherlands were operating at the extreme end of their tethers in East Asia. They had neither the numbers nor a steep enough advantage in technology even to come close to imposing terms on China. Beijing thought them minor irritants at most. They desired formal relations with the Ming court, but the court could find no documentary mention of such far-off places in the available records, and they used that as an excuse to turn them down. Around 1557, the Portuguese gained a residency at Macao for their officials and traders as well as the multinational Jesuits, whom they protected. But that privilege came courtesy of negotiations with the Guangdong provincial officials. Beijing never discussed the concession, or formally endorsed it. Between 1604 and 1624, Ming provincial authorities forcibly pushed Dutch raiders away from the China coast and encouraged them to make their base on Taiwan, a no man's land at the time. The Spanish, similarly, found Manila, which they seized in 1570, as good a base as any from which to engage in China trade. Merchants and émigrés from the Fujian coast swarmed to Manila in great numbers.

It is true that during the century 1550–1650 European traders linked Ming China into an emerging global commercial network, and that this network fed such huge quantities of Japanese and American silver into China as to dramatically affect its taxation system and unbalance its traditional rural economy. Starting in 1555, and continuing to 1640, the Portuguese took advantage of Ming hostilities with the Sino-Japanese coastal raiders and used their own ships to ply unmolested annually between Macao and Nagasaki, trading Chinese silk and other goods for Japanese silver. Meanwhile, the Spanish galleon trade from Acapulco to Manila began operations in 1565, and also focused on silver for Chinese silk goods. Between 1600 and 1657, the Dutch shipped some three million pieces of Jiangxi porcelain to Europe, again in exchange for silver. From 1550 to 1645, the total amount of foreign silver that poured into China from all sources is estimated to have reached some eight to ten thousand metric tons.

It is also true that the Jesuits introduced Western ideas and technology to the court and high bureaucracy; and that the authorities in Beijing, from the Chongzhen emperor on down, were eager to adopt as much of it as they thought would strengthen the country and help defeat the Manchus. Acquiring improved European artillery was a main objective, and the big, accurate new guns were put to some effective use in the field. Interest in other Western things was high, too: Euclidean geometry; improved cartography; astronomy and more accurate calendar making; and European mining techniques, to name a few. But the topic is attractive, and there is a strong temptation to overemphasize all this. None of it saved the Ming, and none of it changed China at all. The Qing dynasty did not pursue European things and ideas with the same eagerness—or perhaps desperation is the right word—as the Ming had shown.[15]

After its fifteenth-century withdrawal from Annam, Eastern Turkestan, Inner Mongolia, and outer Manchuria, the Ming system of frontier management protected China fairly effectively for nearly two centuries. But it was expensive, and its mounting fiscal and human costs could not be sustained forever. The Qing dynasty (1644–1912) managed its frontiers differently. The Manchus as Inner Asians were culturally two-edged, and as Inner Asians used the resources of China to conquer and control the thinly populated expanses of Tibet, Eastern Turkestan, Inner and Outer Mongolia, and Manchuria, thus creating a huge buffer around China and a centrally ruled domain that was not eight times larger than modern France, but eighteen times larger. The Qing probably delivered frontier security that was on the whole cheaper for the taxpayers of China to bear than what the Ming system had required, but the research necessary to prove or disprove the question remains to be done.

CHAPTER TWO

~

Emperors

Any profile of the huge and durable Ming system must shine a light on the sixteen boys and men who, one after the other, were the ultimate decision-makers for it. The final decision in all matters, foreign and domestic, was their responsibility to make. No one could or ever did challenge the emperor's prerogative, or duty, to make decisions. Decisions could be questioned or challenged, but no person or organ could legitimately step in and make decisions in the emperor's behalf. The only way to override the emperor altogether was to declare a new dynasty and forcibly overthrow him. In the mid-seventeenth century, that is just what happened.

Each emperor was different. Each came to power at a different time and faced different choices and difficulties. Their personalities were not the same. Some accomplished big things; others languished, not fit for the task. The procedure here is to take them up one by one. One clue to the puzzle of how the Ming dynasty was able to endure for so long must be looked for in the Forbidden City (*jincheng*), which was, like the White House, both home and office for the ruler, although with all its palace women and eunuchs, the emperors' domicile was by far the larger.

~

The founder of the Ming was a peasant, Zhu Yuanzhang. He is sometimes referred to by his reign title, Hongwu ("vast martiality"), but more often by his posthumous name, Taizu ("grand ancestor"). Taizu is what we will call him here.

The likelihood that the baby born in 1328 to the Zhu family in the drought-stricken and locust-infested flatlands of central China would one day found an enduring regime encompassing all of the Chinese-inhabited East Asian landscape was very close to nil. Taizu was one of six children of a poor peasant tax-evader. An epidemic in 1344 killed off all of the founder's immediate family. Orphaned, unschooled, and lacking resources of any kind, the teenaged Taizu was taken in by a Buddhist temple, issued a robe and bowl, and sent begging for his livelihood. Looking back many years later on his earlier days, the founder himself was amazed at the unlikelihood of what he had accomplished. How could someone of such low estate, "with only my shadow for company," as he put it, ever have risen so high as to become emperor of all of China?

Taizu was a lifelong believer in the power of supernatural forces, shades of the dead as well as the gods and spirits of folk religion, and those forces, bound up in some ineffable way with the ancient idea of a Mandate of Heaven, helped the founder explain to himself and others his absolutely extraordinary success. It was a conviction of divine protection that he had in mind. The founder imposed this religion of his on the whole country, calling it on one occasion the "way of the gods" (*shendao*, the same term as the Japanese *Shintō*). Everywhere, officials central, regional, and local were obliged to conduct seasonal sacrifices and other rites in behalf of the gods of mountains and rivers, of city walls, of the soil and grain. Taizu himself conducted the most solemn sacrifices, to Heaven and Earth. The ruler was well aware that the educated elites of his realm tended to ignore and even scoff at all this, but the ruler, as always, had the final word in the matter. He did not hesitate to inform the world of the reality of this religion and of the seriousness of his intent to compel its observance. Taizu's belief in this mainly civic religion sat easily with his concurrent insistence upon the truth of the "Three Teachings" (*san jiao*): Confucianism, Daoism, and Buddhism.

It all came about this way. Mongol-ruled China began to disintegrate in 1351. Seventeen years of civil disorder followed. Until 1354, religious sectarians were the main leaders of the empire-wide rioting that started it all. Around 1352, a rich fortune-teller by the name of Guo Zixing recruited a band of young men and occupied the central China town of Haozhou (later Fengyang, in northern Anhui province). In April 1352, Zhu Yuanzhang, by now age twenty-three, joined him. By virtue of his inborn intelligence and his determination, he soon won Guo's favor and became the most effective of his officers, not only in devising strategy but also in recruiting other peasants, fellows like himself, to the cause. That same year, Guo gave him a girl to marry, a nineteen-year-old refugee who had been placed in his care, perhaps as a servant. This girl, the future Empress Ma, appears to have been able to read and write. She would go on to serve her extraordinary young husband as an advisor, secretary, and house-manager. In 1355 she gave birth to their eldest son, the future heir apparent, Zhu Biao.

In that same year, 1355, as Yuan rule collapsed, Taizu's star rose yet further as several of his rivals died in the fighting, and his patron Guo Zixing himself died. The future ruler led a large army south out of the battered central region of China and across the Yangzi, capturing the city now known as Nanjing ("southern capital") in 1356. Nanjing became his capital, and it remained as such until Yongle made Beijing the capital in 1420.

The institutional order of this embryonic Ming dynasty was complex. It melded folk customs and traditions alongside the learned elite doctrines and models in which Taizu was always extremely interested. The folkish context included the millenarian Buddhist regime based back in central China that Taizu, making no claims at this stage to independence, served as merely a regional military official until as late as 1366. This was the Great Song dynasty, whose rebel (anti-Yuan) emperor claimed descent from the Song imperial house that had fallen to the Mongols in 1279, and who simultaneously radiated a divine aura as a sort of harbinger for a hoped-for reappearance in the world of the Maitreya Buddha. The folk tradition also featured personal leader-follower bonds that tied the founder to his top lieutenants; they or their sons he married to his many daughters, and their daughters he married to his many sons. He himself adopted orphans as foster sons and used them to carry out espionage and other sensitive missions. Such was the world of the founder's youth, and while he outgrew it, it remained the world of most of his military followers.

Taizu was an autodidact, and from all the signs, extremely intelligent. He actively sought out men of education who could advise him about how to acquire and use power, how to think about what he needed to do in order to become a commanding figure and a founding emperor. Obscure pedagogues of limited knowledge and renown advised him at first, but they knew of others better informed; and as early as 1360, Taizu attracted to his cause Liu Ji and several other south China literati from Zhejiang province who were intellectual heavyweights, in the vanguard of the Confucian intelligentsia nationwide. There is no question but that the founder's ability to recruit such figures and make constructive use of their ideas was one essential key to his ultimate success. But there was much more to the story.

Folk traditions and Buddhist messianism prevailed in the earliest stages of building what would become the Ming, but Confucian precepts and slogans soon supplied an overarching purpose and guiding vision and reassured the educated elites of a battered and war-torn China that Zhu Yuanzhang was not just another run-of-the-mill warlord, but a man of destiny who might well come to rank among the greatest who had ever founded dynasties in the whole long history of China.

Indeed, Taizu was by talent and inclination not so much a warrior as he was an administrator, a chief engineer of human systems; and in this respect he drew upon a fund of ideas and precedents that might perhaps be called Legalist (after the so-called Legalist school of the fourth and third centuries B.C.E.), but which also stemmed from the world of practical affairs that he probably learned from everyday experience and from consultations, not books. Somewhere he made the discovery that no human being was completely trustworthy, no one was above suspicion of corruption and treachery, and that therefore all of the civil and military institutions of the emerging dynastic state had to be configured in such a way that collusion was made very difficult; that parts were kept separate (he forbade military men to consort with literati, for example); and that any one organ was set against all the others in such a way as to ensure that only Taizu could make decisions, ascertain whether his decisions were obeyed, and inflict cruel tortures and death for disobedience or any other kind of malfeasance. In fact his troops were remarkably well disciplined, his civil appointees mostly honest, and there was little of the wanton massacres such as the Qing conducted in the course of their conquest of China in the seventeenth century, nor any of the high-level treachery in his conquest machine that the Qing faced in the War of the Three Feudatories against their former friends and allies. No warlord opponent of Taizu's could compete effectively against him. It was his victory in this competition, not fighting the forces of the crumbling Yuan dynasty, that, Taizu asserted, won him the Mandate of Heaven. The field was swept clean of all opposition. This was as indisputable a claim to legitimacy and power as was ever made in the course of founding a dynasty in the whole history of China.

Taizu became one of the most powerful men ever to rule anywhere, not just in China. He stood atop a war-battered society that could put up little besides passive or token resistance to him. He held Heaven's Mandate, of that he had no doubt. Intellectually he understood himself to be the legatee and defender of all of China's legitimate religions and other bodies of ideas. All of these had something of value to offer rulers who struggled, as he did, to command, control, and rescue humankind from the mindless social and moral corruption that the preceding dynasty had been unable to handle. On top of that, Taizu had his own personal insights, born of experience, to contribute to the solving of large problems. During his thirty-year reign he personally composed a sizeable corpus of tracts and essays in which he strove tirelessly to explain himself and his purposes to the world. No other ruler before Mao Zedong ever produced such a body of written work.

The scope of Ming Taizu's vision and reach was utterly astounding. Absolutely everything fell within the orbit of his competence to judge and manage. Religion? Yes, the ruler sought on a number of occasions to define and regulate that. Foreign policy? Strictly outlined by him as well. Taizu permitted no Chinese to venture abroad, and he channeled all foreign contact with China to the tight controls of the tributary system. The economy? A command economy, of course. The ruler favored village-based peasant agriculture and cloth production and disfavored commerce and specialized manufactures. In the Yuan, the lower Yangzi region (Jiangnan) was the national center of commerce and manufacture, the richest part of China. From 1356 to 1367, Zhang Shicheng, a major warlord rival, had occupied Jiangnan. Upon his defeat of that rival, Taizu proceeded deliberately to destroy the Jiangnan economy. This meant massive deportations of affluent households to the depopulated flatlands of central China, the founder's home region. It involved the imposition of punitive rates of taxation upon the households that remained, as he suspected them of disloyalty. It also involved the slaughter of many thousands of the Jiangnan elite in the great purges of his reign. Prices collapsed nationwide. National income shrank. So did cities. A fiat paper currency was issued, but soon proved worthless. Peasants were told to plant fiber crops. Taxes were ordered to be paid in kind and in labor services.

And what of his governing apparatus? This had a military side, a civil side, and something akin to special operations staffed by eunuchs and palace police. All of this he viewed as purely instrumental, without a shred of independence or self-standing legitimacy, and therefore ready to be cut and contained and shredded in any way that suited the ruler's supreme purposes. Taizu carried out restructurings both small and large, and quickly purged all those whom he found recalcitrant or corrupt or treasonous, both singly and in big purges involving tens of thousands of victims. Most famous was his erasure in 1380, permanent as it turned out, of the office of prime minister, and the prolonged process of ferreting out and destroying everyone even remotely connected to its last incumbent, Hu Weiyong. Then there followed the Stalin-like destruction of virtually the entirety of the top-level military men who had years earlier participated in the founding of the dynasty. Grim reshufflings of offices, the chopping and mincing of provincial civil administration and of the military command hierarchy, were all part of the picture too. And the civil service examination system? Taizu reinstituted it in 1370.

Then he professed profound disappointment in the low quality of the men who managed to pass it. So in 1373 he scrapped it in favor of a system based on personal recommendations. Then in 1385 he restored the exams. But his restless search for new ways to find obedient and honest men of high quality went on and on to the end of his long reign.

Taizu's reach extended downward through the various layers of provincial and local bureaucracy to village level, which it had to do, because the founder did not trust his officials and considered it his personal, Heaven-guided mission to remold all of China's people in line with the ancient ethical norms handed down from the Golden Age of Antiquity. To prevent a repeat of the horrors that brought on the collapse of the Yuan dynasty, nothing less would do. Taizu had spent his early youth at village level, and he thus thought he understood clearly what he was dealing with. But alas, here too every approach of his seemed to come to naught, and so every few years he found himself obliged to reconfigure the system. Who at village level could be trusted? Local magistrates? Elders? Schoolteachers? Affluent landowners? Clergy? Taizu sincerely approached them all, but all proved to be riddled with corruption. Where were the honest people? How does one find them? How can moral instruction be delivered so as to transform evil minds? The founder never gave up. He was still searching for solutions when he died in 1398. His final attempt at a method was to organize village-level schools in which children were taught to memorize his horrifying *Great Announcements* (*Da gao*), which Taizu wrote himself and in which he described in grisly detail the endlessly mindless sins of his people, the terrible punishments he was reluctantly forced to inflict upon them, and the frustration he felt at the recalcitrance and defiance his subjects continued to express despite his sincere efforts to teach and change them.

It is difficult to pinpoint what influence Taizu had on later generations. Recent scholarship has rightly doubted whether the founder imposed an institutional straitjacket on the country because Ming China so clearly evolved beyond much of the despotic harnessing that he placed on it. Taizu left behind no ironbound legacy because his own rulings and writings were inconsistent. Newly enthroned emperors, far from believing that filial piety demanded a continuation of their deceased fathers' policies, regularly used the occasion to announce major policy reversals. Late Ming commercial growth and prosperity owed nothing to Taizu's agrarian principles and anti-commercial instincts. And the list goes on. But the Ming did remain to the end as an emperor-driven system.

The issue of the founder's influence in the long term is complicated by the fact that his was, as he well knew, a unique case, a man whose rich life experiences could never be replicated by any of his palace-bred successors. One rule he legislated was an ironbound rule of primogeniture. No exceptions allowed, and no provisions made for child emperors or emperors who died without sons of their own. It was a poorly thought-out rule, and it had to be circumvented in later generations.

Taizu himself had twenty-six sons. The oldest was Zhu Biao. Portraits of him as a young boy show an appealing child with an abnormally large head. Though he had none of his father's hard edge, Taizu was very fond of him. He had the advantage of an excellent education, which his father had not. Taizu saw to it that the young man became familiar with government and was well prepared for a future role as Ming emperor. Then Zhu Biao died of some unknown malady in 1392, at the age of thirty-six.

It was reasonable inference from the rule of primogeniture, but not a contingency covered by specific house law, that determined that the succession should go next to Zhu Biao's oldest surviving son, and not to any of his many younger brothers. So five months after Zhu Biao's death, Taizu made fourteen-year-old Zhu Yunwen his heir apparent. Zhu Yunwen shared his father's mildness and studiousness. And he was young and very vulnerable, which most likely prompted his grandfather to protect him by destroying thousands of top military officials in the Lan Yu case of 1393. Zhu Yunwen was twenty years old when he assumed the throne upon his grandfather's death five years later, in 1398.[1]

Taizu seems to have known that Zhu Yunwen could not and ought not to try to rule with an iron fist. Indeed the title for the new reign was Jianwen ("establishing civility"), signaling a sharp shift away from Hongwu, or "great martiality." Jianwen's literati advisors urged this shift. But whereas Taizu had always held the upper hand over his advisors, even while he respected their advice, it appears Jianwen, because of his youth and personality, may not have had this advantage. At all events, the new emperor proceeded to terminate his grandfather's increasingly counterproductive policy of national sociomoral reform and lay aside the machinery of punishment and terror that had sustained it for so long. Greater local autonomy was promised; institutions at all levels were to be recharged with legitimacy; and trust was to replace suspicion as a working principle of human relations.

It is uncertain to what extent these new measures were ever carried out. One major reform proved tragically fatal. That was the Jianwen court's effort to put an end to the awkward system of armed princedoms headed by the founder's sons and placed at strategic locations along the frontiers of the realm, especially in the north. Their job was to serve as the military bulwarks of the realm, given Taizu's destruction of most of his senior generals in the purge of 1393. But then Taizu didn't fully trust his sons either; fearing a possible coup, he forbade them to appear together in the capital, Nanjing, for his funeral.

As of 1398, seven of the twenty-six sons had already died. Of the nineteen who were still alive, a half-dozen were still young children. That left thirteen. Six never got involved in the imminent civil war. That left seven. The authorities began summoning them one at a time to come to Nanjing to answer charges of misbehavior. One of his own sons charged Zhu Su, Prince of Zhou, with treason. He was arrested at his garrison in Kaifeng in Henan province, taken in custody to Nanjing, deprived of all privileges, and exiled to Yunnan. Zhu Gui, Prince of Dai, posted at Datong on the northern frontier, was a violent and greedy fellow, and had taken part in military campaigns in Mongolia under the command of his older brother, the Prince of Jin, now deceased. Somehow he was easily placed under arrest and deprived of his princedom early in 1399. Zhu Bo, Prince of Xiang, garrisoned at Jingzhou (now Jiangling, in Hubei province), noted for his riding and shooting skills, also loved learning. He had taken part in a campaign in what is now Guizhou province. In 1399 he was accused of treason. Investigators were sent from Nanjing to check into the charge. The prince panicked. He set fire to his residence, and he and his whole family died in the inferno. Zhu Fu, Prince of Qi, posted at Qingzhou (now Yidu in Shandong province), a violence-loving fellow, had taken part in campaigns into Mongolia. Charged with an intent to rebel, he was arrested like the Prince of Dai without incident, brought to Nanjing, deprived of his princedom, and imprisoned. Zhu Zhi, Prince of Liao, was called back to Nanjing from his recently fortified base at Guangning in southern Manchuria; he arrived by sea, but was cleared of charges, and reassigned as prince to Jingzhou where his brother Zhu Bo had just committed suicide. Zhu Hui, Prince of Gu, based at Xuanfu on the northern frontier, abandoned his post and fled of his own volition to Nanjing. Zhu Bian, Prince of Min, stationed far away in Yunnan, was denounced, cashiered, and exiled for reasons unspecified.

Thus late in 1398 and early in 1399, six princes were unseated from their princedoms. The Jianwen court's apparent idea was to deprive Zhu Di, Prince of Yan, posted at present-day Beijing, of likely allies in a planned confrontation with him, and to do it in such a way as not to arouse his suspicions. That the court tried hard to allay his suspicions may be seen in its agreement to return to him his three sons who were in effect being held as hostages in Nanjing. But war broke out soon after, probably deliberately provoked by the court. A low-ranking commander in the prince's service came to Nanjing and accused Zhu Di of plotting rebellion. Two centrally appointed officials assigned to the Yan princedom were instructed to enter Zhu Di's palace and arrest him. This they tried to do on August 6, 1399. They failed.

Zhu Di, at age thirty-nine the oldest surviving son of Taizu, an experienced commander who enjoyed the loyalty of most of his troops, had been nervously awaiting such a moment. His guards ambushed and killed the two officials as they entered his palace gate. The future city of Beijing was then secured, and within days, nearby cities. Zhu Di issued a declaration of war. His announced aim was not to depose Jianwen, but to purge his evil advisors who were making him do things in violation of Taizu's policy guidelines.

There was still one regional power-wielding prince: Zhu Quan, Prince of Ning, based at Daning, about 150 miles north of Beijing in present-day Inner Mongolia. This prince was twenty-one years old. He had some campaigning experience, and his troops were reputedly fierce fighters. The court at Nanjing had summoned him, but he failed to answer, so the court ordered him deprived of his three guards units. Zhu Di had to act. Leaving his own twenty-one-year-old eldest son (the future Hongxi emperor) in charge of his princedom, he led in person a carefully designed raid on Daning, and brought the Ning Prince's guards as well as the prince himself under his own command. Out in the steppes north of the Yan princedom, the Uriyang-khad Mongols became Zhu Di allies. Daning was then abandoned to them as a reward. The whole operation gained Zhu Di perhaps as many as eighty thousand Chinese and Mongol troops, which he led in a successful relief of Jianwen's siege of the Yan princely seat in December 1399.

So the rebellion was on. Until the summer of 1401, the fighting was mainly confined to an area around present-day Beijing. The Jianwen side held the overwhelming military advantage. In the summer of 1401, Zhu Di struck southward, targeting the capital, Nanjing. He avoided taking the central forces head-on. Prearranged acts of treachery helped smooth his progress. On July 3 of the following year, 1402, he reached and crossed the Yangzi and commenced an encirclement of the capital. Negotiations were opened with a pro-peace Nanjing faction that proposed dividing Ming China in two, the north to be ruled by Zhu Di, the south by Jianwen. Zhu Di would have none of it. He insisted that he just wanted to enter Nanjing to visit his father's tomb. How could they deny him such a simple gesture of filial respect?

In charge at one of the city gates was the Prince of Gu, Zhu Hui, Taizu's nineteenth son, who had fled from his base in north China in 1399. It was he who on July 13 authorized opening the gate. In came Zhu Di, Prince of Yan, on horseback together with some thousand of his troops.

And now the dynastic order of Ming China suffered a shock and upheaval whose reverberations were for many years covered over but never forgotten. Zhu Di's first move was to see that his brothers, Zhu Su, Prince of Zhou, and Zhu Fu, Prince of Qi, were safely released from imprisonment. They were restored to their princedoms, as were all the other accused brothers. The Ming princely establishment thus escaped its impending destruction.

Then it was reported that the imperial palace was on fire! Who set the blaze? No inquiry was ever launched. The bodies of Jianwen's empress and one of his sons were later found in the charred wreckage. The other son, a baby, was rescued, but placed under house arrest (he was released in 1457). No certain trace of Jianwen was ever found, although various legends had it that he had somehow escaped.

The disappeared emperor, together with his reign title (Jianwen), were both expunged from the official records. Zhu Di was in total control of China. The disappeared ruler, he declared, had not been Taizu's legitimate successor. He and his evil advisors had usurped power at the time of the founder's death in 1398. The founder all along had intended that his oldest surviving son, his fourth, Zhu Di, should succeed him! The Jianwen era (Jianwen 1 through Jianwen 4, 1399–1402) was retroactively erased and renumbered Hongwu 32 to 35, continuing the era name used by Taizu. Zhu Di's birth mother was officially stated to be the empress Ma, although it is more likely that Zhu Di was actually the son of a Mongol or Korean concubine. History was officially rewritten to reflect all these newly revealed facts. Starting in 1403, the era name was proclaimed to be Yongle, "everlasting joy." Zhu Di, Prince of Yan, thenceforth came to be known as the Yongle emperor. We will simply call him Yongle.

Yongle's four-year war for the throne left much destruction in its wake in north China. And then there took place in Nanjing a horrific slaughter, amounting to thousands and perhaps tens of thousands of civil officials together with their friends and family members, who stood loyally by Jianwen and defied the usurper (only several generations later was it safe to retell their stories). The military was spared the bloodbath. But once the massacre was over, it was over—unlike Taizu's purge of Hu Weiyong and his adherents that went on for sixteen years. Yongle decided that what China needed was not more bleeding, but rather a virtual orgy of furious emperor-directed activity.

Thus began a whirlwind of new departures, as several giant projects got going simultaneously. One of Yongle's earliest big decisions was to make Beijing the dynasty's main capital and garrison city, leaving Nanjing as a secondary capital with many of the same institutions as before, only reduced in size and authority. The labor and materials costs of building Beijing were colossal. On top of that, huge outlays were required to rebuild the Grand Canal supply line, because the local environment was too poor ever to allow Beijing to live off local resources. The move was decided upon very early, but Yongle himself didn't live there until 1414, and not until 1420 was it formally declared to be the "northern capital" (Beijing).

Yongle redrew the institutional system of Ming China. The founder's pre-occupations with treason, corruption, and national ethical reform continued to be toned down. Instead, Yongle focused his attention on a number of organizational problems. The Ming army with its 2.8 million soldiers was re-tooled in four main ways, as Edward L. Dreyer has pointed out. The princes, though rehabilitated, were with minor exceptions deprived of their guards units and thus of any further role to play in the Ming defense system. Second, guards units were heavily concentrated in Beijing. Third, infantry, cavalry, and artillery camps were set up in Beijing to train troops from all parts of the realm by rotation; and finally, defense outposts that Taizu had placed far out in the Mongolian steppes were pulled back to the line later demarcated by the Great Wall, and the foundations were laid for what later came to be called the nine border defense commands (*jiu bian*). Civil bureaucracy was reshaped as well, especially at the top, where a board of advisors called the Grand Secretariat resumed some of the lapsed functions of the prime minis-ter's office, abolished for all time in 1380. The examination system was made a permanent institution, and it soon became the overwhelmingly preferred path of entry into government service. A system of elite traineeships (the *shujishi*) peeled off the thirty or so top examination degree winners (*jinshi*) and assigned them to the prestigious Hanlin academy. These traineeships later on became a stepping-stone to high central posts, including especially the Grand Secretariat.

In the Yongle era (1402–1424) and for a long while afterward, in great contrast to the high turnover of Taizu's era, officials at the central level held their posts for long periods of time, which contributed to a sense of stability. The examination system came to demand rigid adherence to a fixed intellec-tual orthodoxy, the Cheng-Zhu school of Neo-Confucianism, as embodied in two massive study guides, the *Xingli daquan* and the *Wujing sishu daquan*, published in 1415 and distributed to each of the thousand and more prefectural and county schools of the realm for examination candidates to master. Freelance interpretations of the Confucian classics, possible earlier, were violently suppressed, starting in 1404. More than two thousand students, who if idle might have agitated against the Cheng-Zhu orthodoxy, were put to work on the gigantic *Yongle dadian* project, which aimed to gather and recopy every acceptable text in every field that had ever been written. The work, too large to print, was completed in 1408. Yongle also readjusted and enhanced the role of two important components of rule, the eunuch corps and the investigative police force known as the Embroidered-Uniform Guard (*jinyi wei*). Both agencies enlisted large numbers of non-Chinese: Annamese (north Vietnamese), Mongols, Jurchens, and Koreans. Besides their mundane roles as palace staff, eunuchs leavened both the civil and military sides of Yongle's ruling apparatus: as diplomats, army overseers, naval commanders, emissaries, and spies. In 1420, Yongle placed a check on the espionage and investigative powers of the Embroidered-Uniform Guard when he set up the Eastern Depot, a eunuch-run agency that performed many of the same functions. At some point, perhaps from the outset, the Guard policed the official class, while the Depot handled commoners. The above arrangements lasted through the whole rest of the Ming.

Yongle's spectacular foreign adventures ended shortly after his own death in 1424. It is questionable whether any of them enhanced Ming China's stature and security in the long run. As noted in the previous chapter, Yongle sent embassies to such places as Nepal, Tibet, Herat, Samarkand, Nurgan, Korea, and Japan to reconnoiter, conduct gift exchanges, and enlist foreign states and their rulers as tributaries or at least friends. The biggest moves in terms of size and expense were the annexation of Annam, the six flotillas sent to Southeast Asia and beyond, and six campaigns into the deep steppes of Mongolia, five of them led by Yongle himself. He shifted his attention from south to the north when his new capital at Beijing was made ready. He lost interest in Annam and devoted his attention to Mongolia. His Mongol expeditions, at first conducted every five years, became annual affairs in 1422. At the same time, Zheng He's fleets left China for parts abroad every two years until 1413, when their frequency fell to once every four years. The total fiscal cost of all Yongle's foreign and domestic endeavors is impossible to calculate because there was no central budget, because the military was largely self-supporting, and because so much procurement of labor and materials (such as timber for palace and ship construction) was simply commandeered rather than paid for out of tax revenues. But by one estimate, yearly costs may have run two or three times higher than annual revenue. Such a forced rate of imperial consumption could not have been sustained for much longer.[2]

Yongle died at the age of sixty-four in the summer of 1424, while returning from the last of his Mongolian campaigns. His oldest son, Zhu Gaozhi, was not his favorite son, but in accordance with house law—Taizu's *Ancestral Instructions*—he was made heir apparent in 1404, and twenty years later he succeeded his father. He chose as his reign title the slogan Hongxi ("great brilliance"). Described as having been "fat and sickly," unlike his two robust brothers, he ruled China for eight months only, and died, perhaps of a heart attack, in May 1425.

Hongxi came to power at age forty-six. He had administrative experience, having served as deputy emperor during his father's long absences on campaign. As emperor, he at once undertook a radical reversal of most of his father's policies, mainly with a view to cutting expenses and ending Yongle's aggressive posture toward the larger world beyond. A scheduled departure of Zheng He's fleet was canceled. Requisitions for construction timber and precious metals were curtailed. Surviving relatives of the Jianwen martyrs of 1402 were released from exile or slavery. Much attention was paid to fixing problems that had accumulated in internal administration. Hongxi died just as he was preparing to leave Beijing and move the national capital back to Nanjing. His son Zhu Qizhen succeeded him. The decision to move the capital was then revoked, and never resuscitated.[3]

Zhu Qizhen adopted the reign title Xuande ("spreading virtue"). A high point in the administrative history of the Ming was reached under him, partly due to the fortunate circumstance that Mongolia was fairly quiet during his reign (1425–1435), but Xuande deserves credit for his competence and fair-mindedness. He was born in 1399, and soon became Yongle's favorite grandson. It has been plausibly maintained that the reason why Yongle did not depose Hongxi as heir apparent in favor of Zhu Gaoxu, the younger son he much preferred, was because of his special fondness for this grandchild. Indeed, in 1411 he took the step of designating the child Xuande as "heir apparent to the heir apparent" (*huang taisun*). He kept this grandson in his personal entourage, saw to his education and military training, and had him accompany his trips to Beijing and his campaigns into Mongolia. Thus when Hongxi died, Xuande, by now twenty-six years old, was able to slip smoothly into harness and assume command of the realm.

Xuande was effective as a commander in the field. As soon as he came to the throne, his uncle Zhu Gaoxu—a petulant and disorganized man and a thoroughly bad egg—decided to emulate his father Yongle and start a princely rebellion against his young nephew. Xuande was urged by one of his grand secretaries to take personal charge of an army of suppression. Xuande did so. An army was rapidly assembled. A siege of the prince's fort in Shandong province in 1426 followed. A loud display of cannon fire was enough to make the prince surrender. Xuande had some 600 of his followers executed and another 1,500 sent into exile. The prince and his entire family were imprisoned in Beijing, where later they all died in a fire of unknown origin. The princedom was abolished. There soon arose another occasion for Xuande to show martial prowess. In October 1428, while leading three thousand horsemen on an inspection tour of the steppe frontier, about 150 miles northeast of Beijing, the ruler unexpectedly ran into a party of raiders of the normally friendly Uriyangkhad Mongols and inflicted a defeat upon them. Reportedly Xuande shot three raiders himself with his bow. Xuande staged one of the biggest military parades of all time near Beijing in 1429. A gorgeous painting, still extant, portrays him in Mongol dress, firing a bow from horseback.

Xuande was no militarist, however. The Annam annexation was unraveling badly, Ming forces having suffered a serious defeat, and in Beijing strong voices were raised in favor of a large-scale intervention to retrieve the situation. But in 1427 Xuande turned a deaf ear to their pleas. In 1431, he recognized the rebels as legitimate rulers. It was a controversial decision. Many feared a fatal loss of prestige in the eyes of enemies abroad. It may have been to quell such fears, and reassert Ming paramountcy abroad, that Xuande in 1430 authorized the eunuch Zheng He to conduct for the seventh time his fleet into Southeast Asia and beyond. (Zheng He, in his sixties, died during or not long after returning from this voyage; the fleet idled and rotted away, and nothing like it was ever built again.)

Xuande was aware of some troubling deficiencies in the Ming armies, principally widespread corruption in the hereditary officer corps. He assigned civilian censors to tours of duty to go out and check on the situation in the camps and audit military registers and accounts. He also allowed civil officials to override high-level military officers in the field, by appointing so-called grand coordinators (*xunfu*) to the provinces to have charge of the three offices (regular administration, surveillance, and military) that Taizu had established in 1380 as part of his strategy of breaking up unitary provincial power. Xuande also enhanced the eunuch role in high-level military matters, appointing them as "grand defenders" (*zhenshou*) to serve in tandem with the *xunfu* in the provinces and on the frontiers. Thus Taizu's principle of dividing power was sustained, although in a different way.

Xuande envisioned an enhanced role for civil bureaucracy; and he saw that achieving that goal demanded that the censorial organs be shaken up, purged of poor performers, and severely reminded of their watchdog role. He also had in mind an enhanced role for the palace eunuchs, and to that end he set up in 1426 a palace school for them. At the same time, however, he cracked down heavily on eunuch malefactors. Generally, Xuande wanted national expenses cut, taxes reduced and equalized, relief given to the distressed, and punishments reduced as much as possible.

Yet frugality and restraint did not characterize his personal lifestyle. An artist of some skill himself, he also patronized artists at court. He commissioned the casting of many bronze objects and sponsored a great deal of porcelain production at the kilns in Jingdezhen in Jiangxi province and other places. Ming documents say nothing of this, but Korean records show that Xuande regularly sent eunuchs to the Korean court to demand hunting dogs, falcons, cooks (Xuande liked Korean food), virgins, and yet more eunuchs. These demands eased as soon as he died. Fifty-three Korean girls were repatriated not long after his death.

Xuande died suddenly at the age of thirty-five. He was reported ill on January 20, 1435. He was unable to attend court on New Year's Day, January 29. On the 31st, he died. What killed him is not known.[4]

Ming house law had no provision for what happened next, the accession of a child emperor. Xuande's oldest son, Zhu Qizhen, was eight. The court was forced to improvise. The day before he died, Xuande issued some instructions: the high civil and military officials should guide and assist the child, and they should petition (*bin*) Xuande's mother (Empress Zhang) and the child's mother (Empress Sun) "on all important matters of family and state." Two women would thus wield the imperial decision-making power, until the child came of age. Murky as they may have been, these instructions sufficed to create a kind of makeshift extraconstitutional regency that nevertheless functioned well, inasmuch as the key senior officials had been in high office since the early Yongle era, nearly forty years, and were prudent as well as collegial.

The new emperor assumed the reign title Zhengtong, "upright continuation." He was an appealing child, well loved by his father, who in 1433 had gone so far as to whet his enthusiasm for one day ruling China by having some seven thousand boys brought into the palace as guards whom the future emperor could practice commanding.

After seven years of regency, Zhengtong came of age (fifteen; sixteen by Chinese reckoning) and in 1442 married a Lady Qian as empress. In the same year Zhengtong's grandmother, Empress Zhang, died. She had played a strong hand in the regency, and she had disliked Zhengtong's tutor, the eunuch Wang Zhen, and had been able to restrain his influence. No more. Then in 1446, the last of the famous "Three Yangs," grand secretaries since Yongle's reign, passed away. Their successors as grand secretaries lacked their prestige and steadying influence on the throne. Zhengtong was free to rule as he saw fit.

Unfortunately, the teenager was in thrall to Wang Zhen—as mentor, and probably also a substitute father or elder brother. A file of birthday poems with accompanying congratulatory prefaces attests to Wang Zhen's popularity among favor seekers and some of the high officials in the civil bureaucracy as well. Wang had links to the bureaucracy; he was eager to help his co-provincials from Shanxi, and he wondered aloud, early on, to Chief Grand Secretary Yang Shiqi (from Jiangxi province) why he was seeing so few Shanxi men in high position. Wang Zhen also had vision. It was time, he thought, to restore Ming China's lapsed militarism. At first, this new posture proved successful. Xuande had vetoed a proposed attack on the Shan state of Luchuan on China's southwestern frontier. Now, however, Wang Zhen had Zhengtong authorize full-scale war on Luchuan, under the overall command of a civilian official, Wang Ji (who had years earlier organized the youth guards for Zhengtong as heir apparent). As noted in the previous chapter, this ended in victory in 1449. A different set of civilian-led Ming forces suppressed some large outlaw movements in Fujian, Zhejiang, and Jiangxi provinces (as will be noted further in a later chapter), also in 1449. With these victories to his credit, Wang Zhen next directed the ruler to conduct in person a campaign north into the steppes to take on a new threat, the Oyirad Mongols and their young leader and later khan, Esen. On August 4, a Ming army of some half million left Beijing for an imminent rendezvous with—utter disaster.

Following Yongle's example, Zhengtong left behind in Beijing a deputy emperor to handle routine business while he was gone. This was his younger half brother, Zhu Qiyu, Prince of Cheng. (Zhengtong's own son, the future Chenghua emperor, was only a baby at the time.)

It is something of a mystery why this campaign was so badly organized and led. On September 1, 1449, Esen ambushed the encamped Ming army at a post station called Tumu some seventy-five miles northwest of Beijing and inflicted a horrific slaughter. All the leading generals as well as two grand secretaries and the minister of war were killed, as was the eunuch Wang Zhen. Zhengtong became Esen's personal captive. The debacle would in the long run have far-reaching repercussions on Ming governance, because it severely damaged the institutional prestige of the throne. But immediately, what now?

News of the disaster reached Beijing the next day, September 2. Panic ensued. Fearing the worst, many officials fled Beijing for safety in the south. Some argued that the north should be surrendered to Esen, and the Ming capital relocated to Nanjing, thus dividing China in two, as had happened in the twelfth century, when the Song yielded north China to the Jurchens and reestablished itself at Hangzhou. The counterargument, led by Vice Minister of War Yu Qian, won the day. Ming China must stand and fight. Beijing must be defended. The captive emperor must be deposed in absentia, so that any edict or order coming from him would no longer be valid. His younger brother must become emperor in his place. Otherwise Ming China simply could not function. So on September 22, the change was made. The prince was declared emperor, with the reign title Jingtai ("bright and prosperous"). The first year of Jingtai would begin the first day of the new year (January 14, 1450). Zhengtong was given the title "retired emperor" (*taishang huangdi*).[5]

The new ruler was twenty-two years old, and he had little choice but to make common cause with Yu Qian (promoted to minister of war) and the many other officials who had opposed the eunuch Wang Zhen and the campaign and indeed the whole policy line of revived militarism.

Jingtai was fortunate that Esen had no strategic designs on China other than to force it to liberalize its trade restrictions. Esen delayed an assault on Beijing until late October 1449, which gave Yu Qian enough time to organize an effective defense and reject Esen's demands for a large ransom for Zhengtong. Esen and the former emperor got on well, however. Zhengtong was assigned to live in a comfortable tent compound. But the guest was expensive, and now useless as a hostage. Official negotiators sent out from

Beijing worked out an agreement for Zhengtong's release, and on September 20, 1450, after a year in captivity, he arrived at the Forbidden City in Beijing.

A cold welcome awaited. Freed from one captivity, the hapless ex-emperor immediately entered another, as Jingtai had him and his family put under house arrest, cut off from all contact with the outside world, for the next six years, as things turned out. Meanwhile Jingtai made moves to switch the line of succession, deposing his brother's young son, and naming his own child heir apparent. That was in 1452. The child, however, died in 1453. Jingtai had several other sons. Several officials urged that Zhengtong's son be reinstated as heir apparent. They were flogged to death.

The Jingtai era was appreciated in retrospect as an era of prudent management and good governance on the whole, but the reign was clouded by the anomalous and unhappy situation inside the Forbidden City. Then suddenly it ended. On February 11, 1457, at night and without warning, four hundred soldiers forced their way into the ex-emperor's prison compound. They seized the startled prisoner, placed him in a sedan chair, and carried him to the main audience hall. The coup plotters summoned all the officials to come congratulate their restored emperor. The plotters were a small group carefully self-selected to include representatives of the three main components of Ming rule: the civil bureaucracy, the high military, and the corps of eunuchs. The Jingtai emperor had been for some time too ill to attend court. He was now demoted to his original rank of prince. On March 14, he died. Rumor had it that the palace eunuchs strangled him.[6]

So Zhu Qizhen, the Zhengtong emperor, was restored to power under a new era name—Tianshun, or "heavenly concordance." The restoration began with a big purge of high officials who had served Jingtai. The Minister of War, Yu Qian, for some years a man too sick to work, was arrested, tortured, made to confess to treason (he had saved the Ming in 1449, but no matter). It is certain that Tianshun approved his public execution on February 16, 1457, because Yu Qian had gotten the eunuch Wang Zhen posthumously condemned, his huge properties confiscated, and his close accomplices and family members killed. Tianshun on resuming power honored Wang Zhen with an elaborate Buddhist temple built to commemorate him.

Tianshun never became a puppet of the conspirators who restored him because those men began to plot against each other. Vice censor-in-chief Xu Youzhen, one of the key leaders, was arrested for exceeding his authority, deprived of official status, and exiled to Yunnan in the summer of 1457. Then came the turn of General Shi Heng, probably the most powerful man in China. In 1459, the arrest of his nephew on charges of gross corruption led Tianshun to order his retirement. Imprisonment followed in 1460. The nephew was executed. The general's many relatives and hangers-on were punished, and his extensive properties confiscated. On March 8, 1460, he died of cold and hunger in prison. The eunuch member of the clique, Cao Jixiang (who had had a successful role in warfare in the Zhengtong era), was the last to fall. Under investigation by the Embroidered-Uniform Guard for massive corruption, Cao was driven to desperate measures to save himself. In the summer of 1461, his adopted son led a pre-dawn attack on the Forbidden City, but everything went wrong. The plot had leaked. The attackers burned down a gate, but the intense heat kept them from entering the palace grounds. On August 10, Cao Jixiang was executed, and the enormous properties held by him and his family confiscated. A competent government was, meanwhile, appointed, and the rest of the Tianshun reign was relatively uneventful.

After a short illness, Tianshun died on February 23, 1464, at the age of thirty-six. His oldest son, Zhu Jianshen, age sixteen, succeeded him as the Chenghua ("complete and transformative") emperor.[7]

Young Chenghua had had a difficult childhood during the time of his father's imprisonment. He suffered from a speech impediment and was in no way a commanding figure. But three years after he came to the throne, he was able to handle an unusual situation rather well. His formal mother, Tianshun's principal consort, the Empress Qian, had died childless. Chenghua's birth mother, Empress Zhou, demanded that the woman not be buried alongside Tianshun. That honor, she insisted, was reserved for her alone. Chenghua disagreed with his mother about this, and while as a filial son he could not peremptorily defy his mother, he could and did share his dilemma with the outer court. The issue was not as trivial as it might appear: it was equivalent to an American constitutional crisis over gay marriage, say, with implications for family order all over the country. The bureaucracy, led by Minister of Rites Yao Kui, leapt into action with a mass co-signing by both civil and military officials of petitions in defense of Empress Qian's right to be buried alongside Tianshun. There followed an impromptu mass protest demonstration by much of Beijing officialdom outside the Forbidden City on July 21,

1468. Empress Zhou publicly backed down. Not one voice was raised in her behalf. Key palace eunuchs opposed her, as did Chenghua himself. The final determination was that both empresses might be buried alongside Tianshun. Chenghua was on firm moral grounds remonstrating against a parent who was in the wrong and was endangering the integrity of the ritual and social order of the entire realm.

As the years wore on, Chenghua found ruling China distasteful. His most vexatious duty was making personnel decisions (anyone who has read the diaries of President James K. Polk will understand something of the relentless pressures for preferment and appointment that mid-Ming emperors had to deal with). Chenghua's solution was to withdraw from the fray as much as possible and allow the development of two informal bureaucratic networks, northern and southern, each network with ties to the palace eunuchs, and each geared to promote friends and denounce rivals. Chenghua would tilt first in favor of one group, then shift in favor of the other. It encouraged an atmosphere of cynicism and corruption—and policy drift, exemplified by the initiation of the building of the Great Wall in 1474. After a short illness, Chenghua died on September 9, 1487, at the age of thirty-nine.[8]

Chenghua produced twelve sons and six daughters. His first child, born in 1466 to Lady Wan, died in infancy. Lady Wan, seventeen years older than the emperor, was a murderous dominatrix who obviously initiated the boy Chenghua into the pleasures of sex and kept him in thrall for years thereafter. She was also a thoroughly corrupt businesswoman, who directed eunuchs to scour China for precious goods and accepted payments for the sale of patents of imperial appointment to ambitious officials. Reportedly she had one of Chenghua's other babies killed around 1471. Chenghua thought himself childless until 1475, when a eunuch told him he did have a son, now almost five years old, whom the eunuchs had hidden so as to keep him safe from Lady Wan. This was the eventual Hongzhi emperor. A month after the discovery, the child's mother, a consort from one of the minority peoples of south China, died, perhaps murdered at Lady Wan's direction. No investigation into the matter was ever launched.

Hongzhi (the reign title signifies "great good order") has been justly praised as one of the most conscientious and ethically upright of all of the Ming emperors. He showed as much when at age eighteen he succeeded to the throne and purged the palace and Beijing bureaucracy of relatives of Lady Wan (she had died in 1487), panderers to Chenghua's interests in aphrodisiacs and pornography, and various other unsavory functionaries. (But then he showed a soft spot of his own for the corrupt relatives of his beloved consort, Empress Zhang, declining to restrain them or curtail their outrageous activities.)

Where Chenghua had withdrawn from the everyday grind of governing China, Hongzhi took care to ensure the appointment of good and capable men, and then he worked with them directly, rather than through a variety of shady intermediaries as his father had done. Where Chenghua had favored the military, conferring nobilities and other generous rewards on them, his son preferred to lean in the opposite direction, giving civil officials a leading role in military operations, directing military officers as subordinates. Both reigns featured warfare along the northern frontier, as well as some internal disorder, especially the chaotic situation in the middle and upper Han River region in the years 1465 to 1476 (discussed in a later chapter). Foreign embassies continued to arrive in Beijing, but Ming China now sent no more embassies abroad. On the whole, the Chenghua and Hongzhi eras were a quiet interlude, with troubles but of less than crisis proportions.

The Hongzhi emperor fell ill on June 1, 1505. On June 7, he felt the end was near and called in the grand secretaries to his bedside. He told them that they must help his headstrong and pleasure-loving young son become a good ruler. On the following day he died. He was thirty-four years old.[9]

Since the coup of 1457 that restored Zhu Qizhen to the throne as the Tianshun emperor, a half-century of calm and passivity emanated from the Forbidden City, as Tianshun, Chenghua, and Hongzhi, for all their differences as personalities, were not inclined to do anything new or rash. Zhengde was certainly different. Less a serious reformer than an utter madcap, the physically vigorous, intelligent, but unteachable young ruler threw off all restraint, and for sixteen years mocked every rule and convention that the Ming system had thus far accumulated—not so much in order to reform the system, but rather to live life as he liked and to the fullest. The Ming was an autocracy. Whatever the emperor decided, his decision was in the end valid, because an emperor was his own supreme court. But just how far could he push that prerogative?

Zhengde (the reign title, ironically, means "upright and virtuous") was all of thirteen years old when he succeeded to power in June 1505. From the very outset, his close friendship with a clique of seven eunuchs coupled with his visceral dislike of the high civil officials became clear. At length, in October 1506, many high officials, conscious that the dying Hongzhi had asked them to guide the young Zhengde, staged a large demonstration at the Meridian Gate just outside the Forbidden City. They demanded that the emperor surrender the seven eunuchs to the judicial organs for trial and execution. Feverish negotiations followed. Then eunuch Liu Jin rose to the challenge of the occasion, seized power with Zhengde's blessing, and crushed the demonstration. All the participants in it were purged and blacklisted. A follow-up protest conducted by officials in Nanjing ended in their being brought to Beijing and flogged. For the next four years, until 1510, Zhengde gave Liu Jin free rein to run China.

Liu Jin set in motion some changes, of which one was to remedy corruption, inefficiency, and shortfalls in revenue collection by inflicting heavy punishments on cheats and frauds and by sending eunuch-directed teams of agents out to the provinces to uncover new revenue sources. This drive provoked the 1510 rebellion of the Prince of Anhua, based in Shaanxi province, where mutinous soldiers were among those being hard pressed for taxes. A high civil official, Yang Yiqing, and a palace eunuch, Zhang Yong, were sent with an army to quell the rebellion, which they did easily. Then the two conspired to convince Zhengde that Liu Jin was plotting to assassinate him. Zhengde personally accompanied a search of Liu Jin's residence. The searchers found there a cache of weapons, including a fan that the eunuch often carried in the emperor's presence. It was shown to hide a knife. Zhengde had Liu Jin arrested and turned over to the outer court for prosecution. The trial was perfunctory. Liu Jin was executed by slow slicing. Liu Jin had inflicted bloody lashings on protesting officials in the past; the officials had their own even bloodier revenge on him in the end.

After Liu Jin's execution, eunuchs continued to squeeze the realm for revenues, mainly through sheer extortion. Zhengde meanwhile, now eighteen, shifted his attention to military affairs. For him this was not just an administrative bias, as it had been for his sedentary grandfather, Chenghua, but a desire to take to the field and taste combat in person. His key accomplice in this was a cavalry officer, Jiang Bin, who came to the ruler's notice in 1512, and for the next decade served as his aide-de-camp, and an adopted son as well. Together they remedied Beijing's exposure to increased outlaw activity in north China by bringing down seasoned northern frontier troops and sending untrained capital troops to replace them on the frontier. Zhengde took a personal part in troop training exercises. And then in 1517, over the protests of the high civil officials, he led an army from Beijing to the Xuanfu frontier garrison, a hundred miles to the northwest. There, in a reversal of what had happened at Tumu in 1449, Zhengde encountered a raiding party of Dayan Khan (also known as Batu Möngke, like Esen earlier an important unifier of the Mongol peoples), and in a two-day confrontation, Zhengde and his cavalry forced the raiders to retreat back into the steppes. Right after this, Zhengde hit upon an idea, a clever sort of joke, that he had a double in a general named Zhu Shou. As emperor he would issue orders to this Zhu Shou to conduct this or that operation. The grand secretaries, exasperated, could do nothing to stop this.

Zhengde hated the Forbidden City and had no liking for Beijing either. Around 1507, he ordered construction of a new palace complex called the Leopard Quarter, for its proximity to that part of the imperial zoo. From there, in 1514, the ruler watched in undisguised glee as a fire consumed the main palaces inside the Forbidden City. He liked the garrison town of Xuanfu, and so he began building a palace complex there as well. He ordered up a Mongol-style mobile city of 162 tents in 1515 to accommodate him and his entourage while on the road to and from Beijing.

If his great-great-grandfather Xuande liked Korean girls, Zhengde preferred Muslim girls from east Turkestan (now Xinjiang province). Until, that is, he met the love of his life in a Chinese songstress from Taiyuan in Shanxi in 1518. (He had a formal empress, Empress Xia, to whom he was married a year after his enthronement, but he showed no interest in her.) For all his womanizing, Zhengde never had any children.

He liked Tibetan monks, as had his grandfather Chenghua. He set up special quarters for them in his Leopard Quarter. In 1516 he sent a Ming mission abroad, the first such in many years, to bring back to China the young miracle-working hierarch of the Karma-pa sect in Lhasa; but the huge embassy, led by eunuch Liu Yun, bogged down in gross corruption. The holy monk's protector sent troops to drive the embassy away. It failed utterly to achieve its goal.

March 1519 found Zhengde in Beijing on one of his occasional visits after touring the northern frontier. He prepared to pay a visit to south China, which he'd never seen before. The civil bureaucracy, for years shunted aside in Zhengde's preference for eunuchs and military officers, decided almost to a man to risk their lives and careers in a mass protest. The officials had tried this tactic thirteen years before, to no avail. No matter. They now gathered in a kneeling demonstration at the Meridian Gate outside the Forbidden City (Zhengde was inside) and vowed to stop him with their own bodies. Zhengde and Jiang Bin reacted in fury. Arrests were made. Severe floggings were administered, from which twelve officials died. Zhengde postponed his trip until September.

Then in the summer of 1519 the rebellion of the Prince of Ning, long simmering, broke out. Long before, Yongle had moved the seat of the Ning princedom from Daning on the steppe frontier to Nanchang in Jiangxi province. Zhu Chenhao was a fifth-generation descendant of the original prince, Taizu's seventeenth son, Zhu Quan. A schemer rather than a military man (princely guards units having been abolished long before), the prince worked bribes in his attempt to usurp the throne. This was a tempting opportunity, given that Zhengde was childless. (Bribes had also been key to Yongle's successful usurpation in 1402.) The prince bought allies in the minister of war and some highly placed palace eunuchs. Rumors and then concrete reports of the prince's treason abounded, but Zhengde ignored them. The prince then gathered an army of outlaws, began acting like an emperor, and agitated to get his son invited to Beijing to serve as an heir apparent. But his plans unraveled. Jiang Bin and others showed Zhengde firm evidence of the prince's designs. On July 10, 1519, the prince openly declared Zhengde a usurper, not the actual child of Hongzhi, and launched a campaign northward, aiming to capture Nanjing first. The ragtag princely army reached Anqing prefecture on the Yangzi, well short of Nanjing, but the city defended itself and refused to fall. Wang Yangming, civilian grand coordinator in southern Jiangxi, rapidly assembled an army, captured the unguarded princely seat at Nanchang, destroyed the prince's river-borne army on August 20, and soon after, captured the prince himself.

Meanwhile, Zhengde ordered his imaginary double to lead an army south to crush the rebellion. The day after he and his entourage left Beijing, Wang Yangming's report of the prince's capture reached him. The trip continued anyway. Zhengde reached Nanjing in January 1520, and after an extended and enjoyable stay, returned to Beijing with the captured prince in tow. In January 1521, Zhu Chenhao was ordered to commit suicide.

Whether from alcoholism, or the effects of a fall into cold water from a fishing boat, or some disease, Zhengde felt sick enough to postpone another trip to his palace in Xuanfu. He did not recover from whatever ailed him, and he died in Beijing on April 15, 1521. He was twenty-nine. He named no successor. Now what?[10]

Again, the situation necessitated improvisation. As Yu Qian had done in 1449, so Chief Grand Secretary Yang Tinghe seized the moment in 1521, though in less panicked circumstances. He and Grand Empress Dowager

Zhang (Hongzhi's widow) agreed to call a young Ming prince, Zhu Houcong, up from his base near the Yangzi in Hubei to assume the throne. Exactly why and how they chose him, and not some likelier candidate, was never explained. (He belonged to the same generation as his cousin, Zhengde, Zhu Houzhao, and his recently deceased father was the son of a concubine.) Jiang Bin, Zhengde's top lieutenant, had another prince in mind; but he faltered badly as Yang Tinghe took the initiative and had Jiang and his four sons arrested and executed on July 11. The authorities confiscated his enormous holdings of gold and silver.

The new ruler was thirteen years old on accession, and went on to rule for forty-five years under the reign title Jiajing ("excellent and serene"). He was not a good ruler. Indeed, it says something about the resilience of the Ming system that it somehow endured not just sixteen years of Zhengde's wild behavior, but forty-five years of cruel mismanagement by one of the most self-centered, self-indulgent, short-tempered, and humorless autocrats in the country's history. But Jiajing did understand power. He showed that understanding from the very first, when in May 1521 his cortege reached Beijing and he refused to be admitted to the Forbidden City through a side gate; and again in October when he threatened to abdicate if his mother were not given the title of empress forthwith. Through his long reign, questions of imperial ritual would crowd his agenda. Yang Tinghe engineered the revival of the influence of civil bureaucracy over the eunuchs and military, and Jiajing consistently endorsed that preference, although Yang himself did not fare so well.

As to ritual, the sensational Great Rites demonstration of 1524 was the defining event, the keynote statement of the young ruler's commitment to one side of a thorny issue. Chief Grand Secretary Yang Tinghe and the clear majority of the civil officials believed that ritual required Jiajing in effect to disown his own father and become the son of the Hongzhi emperor by way of posthumous adoption. That would prevent the extinction of the direct line of imperial descent. Jiajing profoundly disagreed. The matter came to a head in the summer of 1524 when nearly all of Beijing officialdom dropped what they were doing and mounted an impromptu demonstration, wailing and kneeling outside the Meridian Gate, placing their careers and lives on the line in an emotionally supercharged effort to compel the ruler to change his mind. The question exploded well beyond its origin in a ritual technicality, and metastasized into a moral-constitutional crisis of the first order, a heated replay of the demonstration of 1468. The protesters insisted that the ruler must put aside personal and selfish matters (filial piety toward his own father) and champion a moral line for the whole realm. The integrity of the imperial succession must trump that of family succession.

Jiajing would have none of that. Instead of ritually disowning his own father, he would instead promote him to the rank of posthumous emperor and in that way both express his sense of filial obligation as well as honor the notion of imperial descent. That is what his feelings told him to do.

What made this demonstration so different from anything that had gone before was that Jiajing also had a genuine intellectual argument on his side. Was ritual merely a matter of observing canonical rules handed down from the past, or was ritual something that must be grounded in human emotions? But if one yields to human emotions, aren't all restraints on excess and misbehavior removed? If one yields to ironclad rules, might not the resulting unhappiness be beyond endurance? Jiajing settled the matter with brute force, but followed it with detailed explanatory propaganda. The protesters were arrested and seventeen of them died of the flogging they got. Yet one large segment of the educated elite, the Wang Yangming school in particular (to be discussed in a later chapter), and even more the people of the realm generally, liked Jiajing's endorsement of feeling at the expense of rules and turned it to their own advantage.

This emotional conjuncture of emperor and people was wholly fortuitous. Jiajing was no populist. Nor did he favor the Wang Yangming school. He had acted solely for himself, hardly thinking of the larger effects of what he was doing.

Young Jiajing was studious. At times he alertly attended the daily lectures and tutorials in the classics and histories that the high officials prepared for him. By 1527 he was concocting his own short texts in Cheng-Zhu Neo-Confucianism. These were carved in stone and set up with great fanfare in schools nationwide. People paid them scant attention. By 1530, however, Jiajing's interest in study waned; he began criticizing and bullying his teachers, and by 1536 he dropped his studies altogether in favor of Daoism and other pursuits.

This change was connected to twists and turns in the fierce partisan battles that were plaguing the now predominant civil bureaucracy. First to suffer the imperial wrath were officials who had stood behind Yang Tinghe in the early days of the Jiajing reign on the losing side in the Great Rites controversy. Next to suffer, in the early 1530s, were Jiajing's supporters, as they fell out among themselves. Grand Secretary Xia Yan then became the chief implementer of Jiajing's wishes. He cheerfully pandered to the ruler's new interest in Daoism, saw to a thorough reordering of the imperial ritual program, and adopted the hard line in the ongoing debate over whether to try to recover the Ordos from its Mongol occupiers. He also favored heavy military retaliation elsewhere along the frontiers. But because Jiajing, on the whole, did not favor military solutions to problems, and because Xia Yan was not careful to keep himself apprised of the emperor's latest wishes, he became more and more of an irritant. The grand secretary paid with his life: he was executed on October 31, 1548. His onetime ally and later rival, Yan Song, now chief grand secretary in his place, helped arrange his demise.

Yan Song took care to please his ruler. He also built up a formidable bureaucratic machine, executed his harshest critics, and did much of the work of governing the Ming from 1548 until 1562, when he at last grew careless, and angered Jiajing by balking at the cost of rebuilding a palace of Jiajing's that had burned down. Grand Secretary Xu Jie urged his dismissal. Jiajing dismissed him. Xu Jie then became chief grand secretary in turn until his own dismissal in 1567, after Jiajing had died. The three—Xia, Yan, and Xu—were, each in his own way, capable men who managed to provide through the long Jiajing reign a modicum of stability and order.

Jiajing took an active part in governance early in his reign, regularly intervening in judicial and other cases in defiance of established laws and procedures. Then on the night of November 27, 1542, eighteen girls tried to strangle Jiajing with a rope while he was asleep in the apartment of a favorite concubine. Their attempt failed, as they didn't tie the right sort of knot. The empress had eunuchs arrest and kill all the girls plus the concubine Jiajing was sleeping with. As soon as he recovered from the trauma, Jiajing moved out of the Forbidden City for good, to an enormously expensive palace complex of his own design in a park to the west of the Forbidden City, in the same general area where his cousin Zhengde's Leopard Quarter had once been. There he took up a lifestyle as the immortal ruler of a Daoist never-never land, a paradise, over which he presided in the close company of Tao Zongwen, a religious adept, ritualist, healer, exorcist, and concocter of potions and elixirs of various sorts, of which the ingredients included body fluids from several hundred prepubescent girls, rounded up periodically so that the ruler might have sexual relations with them exactly at the moment of first menstruation. Elaborate altars to the Daoist God of Thunder, put up in Beijing and elsewhere, seemed to presage the establishment of a new national religion. Jiajing now made decisions on legal and administrative matters only after consulting the Daoist deities through a planchette. Xia Yan, Yan Song, and Xu Jie gained personal meetings with Jiajing by way of their ability to please him by writing Daoist prayers with special ink on special paper. The ruler no longer conducted court in front of all the assembled officials.

Jiajing's deep and sincere feelings for his parents did not extend to any other family members. He had no siblings. Two sisters and a brother had died in childhood, and his father died at age forty-two. We are not privy to

Jiajing's inner fears, but these premature deaths may have led him into his fervent embrace of Daoism and its various life-lengthening recipes. There is no doubt that his long failure to produce an heir led him to Daoism's fertility prayers and aphrodisiacs. It didn't help matters that he abused his empresses. A first empress's jealousy angered him, and she died pregnant in 1528. A second empress shared Jiajing's delight in ritual and ceremony, but she produced no heir and Jiajing deposed her in 1534. She died two years later. A third empress, also childless, died in a palace fire in 1547; Jiajing chose not to send rescuers for her. Eventually, the ruler produced eight sons and five daughters by various secondary wives, but of them only two sons and two daughters lived to become adults.

Possibly it was the arsenic and lead ingredients in the Daoist potions the ruler drank that slowly killed him. By the 1560s he was suffering from insomnia, various skin and stomach ailments, and violent mood swings. He died on January 23, 1566.[11]

⌒

As was often the case with new Ming enthronements, a thorough and refreshing reform of policies and systems accompanied this one. Chief Grand Secretary Xu Jie was responsible for composing the Jiajing emperor's final and self-accusatory instructions. Here in 1566, as with Chief Grand Secretary Yang Tinghe in 1521, the high civil bureaucracy had the leading role at a critical moment in the dynastic succession. Xu Jie released from brutal mistreatment in prison a number of Jiajing's critics and detractors. He restored them to office. He dismantled the whole Daoist establishment. In the years following policy changes of a more far-reaching sort were put into effect—a satisfactory peace agreement with Altan Khan in 1571; an easing of the ban on maritime trade; and an important move to restore morale in the long neglected military establishment, by placing the new Longqing emperor physically at the center of a huge and spectacular parade and review near Beijing in the autumn of 1569.

The Longqing era (the name means "eminent good fortune") was short. Longqing himself was an extremely passive character, and therefore very hard to know. Jiajing had never liked him and refused until as late as 1560 to name him heir apparent, even though he was the oldest surviving son. He was indifferently educated, and some physical or psychological defect prevented his ever speaking in public. He was twenty-nine years old when he became emperor. He seems to have lacked his father's ill humor and penchant for cruelty. The grand secretaries were very much at liberty to establish policy and manage government.

After several months' illness, Longqing died on July 4, 1572. He had four sons and seven daughters; two sons and four daughters survived childhood. His oldest surviving son was his third, Zhu Yijun, known as the Wanli emperor, whose reign turned out to be the longest of the sixteen Ming rulers, forty-eight years from 1572 to 1620.[12]

Wanli (the name means "a myriad of ages") came to the throne at the age of nine. Once again, as in the case of the child Zhengtong in 1435, an improvised regency had to be put together. This one consisted of Wanli's mother, Empress Li; the eunuch Feng Bao; and Chief Grand Secretary Zhang Juzheng. Though only a secondary consort to Longqing, Empress Li was a formidable palace presence, and she remained so down to her death in 1614. Two of her brothers were high-ranking military officials, and a third was a palace eunuch, a situation showing the interlinkages that could develop among non-bureaucratic elites. Wanli, when he came of age, much preferred eunuchs and military men to any of his civil officials—showing what by now had become something of a predictable pattern of imperial preferences for this or that branch of governance. Chief Grand Secretary Zhang, however, enjoyed the strong support of both the empress and Feng Bao and, as is well known, ruled China as virtual dictator, implementing a major program of fiscal retrenchment and other reforms until 1582, when he died in office. In fact, Zhang was the last and most effective in a line of powerful chief grand secretaries that extended all the way back to 1521 and Yang Tinghe.

Zhang was a stern taskmaster, and Empress Li fully backed his efforts to train and forcefully restrain the fatherless child Wanli. Understandably, Wanli came to bear a lifelong resentment against Zhang for his domineering severity. In 1582, he acted on this feeling when he answered the bureaucracy's charges against Zhang by confiscating his property and persecuting the surviving members of his family. No subsequent grand secretary ever came near to wielding such power as Zhang had wielded.

Nor did Wanli ever allow a eunuch or military officer to act as his surrogate, as Zhengde had done first with Liu Jin and then with Jiang Bin. To the end of his life, Wanli, whose health was never good, preferred to stay inside the Forbidden City and rule in person, but from behind the scenes. He was interested in only two things—military and fiscal issues. In fiscal matters, he began in 1596 to augment the revenues available from normal channels with the much larger sums palace eunuchs could gather for him. Palace eunuchs and their gangs of thugs and enforcers descended upon the realm with orders to open mines, as well as extort taxes of all kinds. This income was needed for ever-increasing palace expenses—construction and lavish ceremonies. Wanli insisted that military operations be funded entirely from regular revenue sources and, when necessary, surtaxes, which regular officials were supposed to collect.

Military operations along the thousands of miles of Ming frontier, Mongolia excepted, were the centerpiece of Wanli's long reign. He thus continued a military revitalization that had begun during the short reign of his father, Longqing. The armed forces were once again respected and, often enough, rewarded and honored for their work. Liu Ting, a commander of inherited status, is an outstanding example of a man whose military career piled success on success until disaster struck in 1619. One finds Liu Ting on campaign in Luchuan and Burma in 1582; in Korea, against the Japanese, in 1592 and 1597; then, under the overall supervision of a capable civilian official, Li Hualong, with an important part in the conquest of Bozhou on the southwestern frontier in 1600; then a sad end came when, as leader of one of four large armies on campaign against the Jurchens (later Manchus) led by Nurhaci, his men were scattered and routed and he himself killed in the field in Manchuria on April 7, 1619. (The other three armies were taken by surprise and, never able to coordinate efforts, were also routed.)

Wanli, like several of his predecessors, found dealing with the civil bureaucracy unpleasant. His way of coping with it was to withdraw from direct contact with any of its officials, to respond through eunuch intermediaries only to urgent matters relating to war and finance, and simply to ignore most of the rest. As the years wore on, his strategy led to the slow strangulation of some key functions of the Ming state. As incumbent officials at the central, provincial, and local levels resigned, or simply walked away from their posts, few replacement appointments were made. Judicial appeals were left unanswered. Prisoners languished indefinitely and died in custody, as for want of judges, their cases could not be taken up. What remained of civil government was seriously demoralized. The remaining censorial authorities, themselves riddled by faction, intimidated everyone; a self-styled "good species" (later labeled Donglin) fought self-interested provincial cliques of various sorts. Unquestionably the key issue of contention in this factionalism was nothing directly relating to war or finance, but rather the succession to the Ming throne!

Wanli gave every indication that he preferred a younger son, Zhu Changxun, born of his favorite concubine, Lady Zheng, to his oldest son and rightful successor, Zhu Changluo, born of a different palace lady. The "good species" sent up an unceasing stream of memorials demanding that Wanli formally recognize Zhu Changluo as heir apparent, because the future security of Ming China was at stake in the matter. It was his own mother, Empress Li, who persuaded Wanli that he had to designate formally Zhu Changluo as heir, which he did in 1601. But Zhu Changxun stayed in the Forbidden City, a constant threat to that arrangement. The "good species" protested long and loud, and again Empress Li made her son yield, and in 1614 Zhu Changxun was sent away as Prince of Fu to a lavish palace estate built especially for him at Luoyang in northern Henan province (where he was murdered and his assets seized by the rebel Li Zicheng in 1641). That did not end the succession issue, because the "good species" considered a never fully investigated attack by a lone assailant on the heir apparent's palace in 1615 evidence that Wanli and Lady Zheng were still intent upon changing the succession. Wanli shocked the officials by calling them all to a special meeting inside the Forbidden City and, with the heir apparent and his two grandsons standing right by his side, scolding them for their unfounded suspicions.

Wanli had won wars against Bozhou and against Japan in Korea, but the realm was still reeling from the calamitous military defeat of 1619 in Manchuria when he died on August 18, 1620, at the age of fifty-six. He sired a total of eight sons and ten daughters, of whom only five sons and two daughters survived into adulthood. Wanli's exhumed remains show him to have been about 5'5" in height, with a congenitally bent back.[13]

As often happened in Ming times, a new enthronement was an occasion for a change in policy. The enthronement of Zhu Changluo, age thirty-eight, after nearly a half-century of Wanli's rule, or misrule, involved a policy shift that was quite radical. The "good species," by now commonly identified as the Donglin party, having agitated long and hard for many years to champion the new ruler's rights to the succession, now scored a major triumph. The late summer of 1620 featured the recall of many officials who had been dismissed over the years for protesting Wanli's policies, and swiftly the depleted ranks of the bureaucracy began to fill up once again. Wanli's eunuch mining superintendents and tax commissioners were all recalled from the provinces. Some two million taels silver from the Wanli's personal treasury were issued as rewards and emoluments for the 867,964 soldiers posted along the frontiers. Unlike his father, the new emperor was open to advice and admonition from his officials, and it certainly looked as though an era of rejuvenating change was under way, even in the new government's first weeks. The new era name was Taichang, "prosperous and flourishing."

Then the unbelievable happened. Three days after his August 28 enthronement, Taichang reported feeling unwell. In the days following, he grew weak and dizzy, unable to walk. Medicines of a doubtful sort were given him, to no avail. On September 26, he died. What? People could scarcely believe his demise was natural. What on earth killed him? The Donglin party was absolutely sure that Wanli's favorite concubine, Lady Zheng, had a part in his unexpected death, as had other sinister forces. It then appeared that Lady Zheng and the dead emperor's favorite consort, Lady Li, were about to form a regency to rule in behalf of Taichang's heir apparent, Zhu Youjiao, who was fourteen years old, unmarried, and by Chinese reckoning still a minor. His own mother was dead, and Lady Li's status was shaky. A hot-blooded Donglin partisan, Yang Lian, quickly sprang into action, inspiring and carrying out an invasion of the Forbidden City, normally off-limits to civil officials. Yang and his group captured the young heir and had him proclaimed emperor in his own right in the presence of a hastily called assembly of Beijing officialdom. Thus began the Tianqi ("celestial inception") era, in somewhat of a reprise of the Tianshun affair of 1457. Perhaps the promising dawn that had only just broken under Taichang could continue to brighten into full daylight under his young successor.[14]

Taichang fathered fifteen children, but only five survived, two boys (the Tianqi and Chongzhen emperors) and three girls. The boy Tianqi, physically undersized, uninterested in learning, emotionally dependent upon his wet nurse Madame Ke and her ally, the wily eunuch Wei Zhongxian, seems to have harbored some artistic talent, but was disastrously cast as emperor of an increasingly troubled Ming China. He did continue at first his father's leaning toward the Donglin faction, but the Donglin moral extremists, who had boosted him to the throne, inadvertently helped to alienate the little emperor by their vociferous objections to the continued presence, even after Tianqi's marriage in 1621, of the wet nurse Madame Ke in Tianqi's personal quarters in the Forbidden City. With eunuch Wei's help, Tianqi stood fast. The Donglin attack was blunted.

It soon became clear to Tianqi that he was not capable of ruling by himself, and that his best option was to make palace eunuch Wei Zhongxian, a much older man and a kind of substitute father and protector, a kind of associate emperor, perhaps a Dick Cheney, an arrangement without clear precedent in Ming history. The Donglin faction protested heatedly. In retaliation, Tianqi and Wei conducted a major purge, dismissing hundreds of officials and arresting, torturing, and murdering thirteen Donglin leaders, including the firebrand Yang Lian. Henceforth, all memorials to the throne had to include favorable mention of the eunuch, and all rescripts from the palace were issued jointly in the name of the emperor together with the "depot minister"—Wei's official title as head of the Eastern Depot, the eunuch-run police and investigation agency.

A mood of sycophancy spread through the realm, as pro-Wei officials were appointed to replace the purged Donglin. In many of the key cities, local elites and officials built lavish shrines in Wei Zhongxian's honor. For a moment, however, the new order showed some promise. In 1626, after years of defeat in Manchuria (the debacle of 1619 was followed by a further collapse of Ming armies there in 1621), Ming forces managed to reconquer the garrison town of Ningyuan (now Xingcheng, on the coast about 250 miles northeast of Beijing) and beat back a counterattack by Nurhaci. Back in Beijing, Wei was happy to claim full credit for the victory.

Tianqi liked boating, watching puppet shows, horse races, and military exercises. Wei Zhongxian was eager to help entertain him, and relieve him of many of his administrative duties. In 1627, Tianqi became gravely sick, and whatever the disease may have been, it took his life on September 30, 1627. He was twenty-one. He had fathered five children. All of them died in infancy. On his deathbed, Tianqi did act to ensure the transmission of the throne to his younger half brother, Zhu Youjian, sixteen years old. That the ultimate authority belonged to Tianqi, not to Wei Zhongxian, was clearly shown here. Wei and Madame Ke had no connection to, or liking for, the emperor-designate.[15]

The last emperor of an intact Ming China ruled under the reign title Chongzhen ("estimable and fortunate"). Despite his very young years, he was studious and earnest and would have nothing to do with any surrogates.

He was intent upon taking an active personal part in government. Under his direction, Wei Zhongxian was dismissed. He committed suicide (as did his chief ally in the bureaucracy, Cui Chengxiu, censor-in-chief and concurrent minister of war). A partial purge of high-level officials followed, after careful investigation: 161 men were punished or dismissed, and of them, 24 men were sentenced to death. Many of the Donglin party were pardoned and recalled to office.

However, this was far from a complete victory for the Donglin, and far from a complete vindication of their moralizing political stance. Chongzhen met regularly with the officials, and he made it clear to them that there would be no thorough purge, that China was beset with serious troubles on many fronts, and that it was time to put all partisan infighting aside and work together to save the realm. His scolding was right on the mark. However, so toxic had the political atmosphere become that no one heeded him. Chongzhen tried to conduct a balancing act between the factions, but that only exacerbated the strife. Appointees to high office came and went at a dizzying pace. In desperation, Chongzhen turned more and more to eunuchs to conduct important military and other tasks.

In times that were less stressed, Chongzhen would have fared well as a ruler. He much resembled the well-remembered Hongzhi emperor in his willingness to involve himself constructively in the work of government. But the times were against him. It was nothing new for Ming government to have to deal with an array of serious problems: floods, droughts, famines, revenue shortfalls, currency crises, corruption, wreckage along the Grand Canal and Great Wall, troop mutinies, frontier wars and disturbances, piracy, princely uprisings, internal mass migration, outlawry—on and on. In the 1550s, Mongol raids reached as far as Beijing, while deep pirate raids threatened Nanjing in 1555–1556. Had the Sino-Japanese raiders and the Mongols fought in concert—or even better, had either or both of them aimed at permanent occupation and political takeover—then the Ming as an intact dynasty might have ended with Jiajing. Or with Zhengtong in 1449, had the Oyirad Mongol Esen pressed the advantage he held. Chongzhen was a much better ruler than either Jiajing or Zhengtong. It was his bad luck to be overwhelmed by too many serious problems at once at a time of bureaucratic infighting and partisan dysfunction. At the same time, an external enemy, the Manchus, was no longer content with raiding and was, with the help of Ming military and civilian defectors, building a conquest machine. Internal outlaws, Li Zicheng and Zhang Xianzhong, were likewise turning from raiding to founding would-be dynasties.

It was Li and his Shun dynasty forces who took Beijing in 1644, and left a by-now berserk Chongzhen no good option he could think of other than suicide. On April 25, 1644, he hanged himself. To the end, he considered himself not to blame for the disaster; it was his officials who had failed him. Li held Beijing for a little over a month. Then the Manchus and their ex-Ming allies chased him out, and commenced a conquest of all of China that would take them half a century to complete.

As a coda for this chapter, we can ask ourselves what sort of contribution the Ming emperors overall made to the endurance of the Ming system. A shrinking contribution seems clear. After the first half-century or so, it seems to become a matter of indifference what sort of ruler ruled China. The system carried on through long periods of bad rule, only to fall apart, rather ironically, during the reign of an emperor who was involved and capable. Had excellent emperors prevailed throughout, would Ming China perhaps have lasted twice as long as it did, say down to the twentieth century? Or was the Ming likely to collapse sometime during the seventeenth century in any event? The Qing (1644–1912) lasted 268 years, almost exactly as long as the Ming, and featured nine emperors, of whom the first six were good administrators enjoying comparatively long tenures. The quality of the Qing emperors was, on the whole, decidedly superior to that of their Ming counterparts. Yet the Qing imperial center was scarcely operative after 1850, and its earlier legacy of effective rule could not prevent its deterioration and final collapse in 1912. I would hypothesize that not even a long succession of wise and competent rulers would have sufficed to steer Ming China over the shoals of the seventeenth century. Later I'll try to explain why.

CHAPTER THREE

Governance

To analyze a collapse is a fairly straightforward challenge. To explain how a system such as the Ming survived for close to three centuries is not so easy. It helped that Ming China's geographical setting in East Asia was of a certain shape—round and compact. It helped that along its five thousand miles of land frontier lived non-Chinese societies of much smaller population size, whose ability to project power into China was mainly limited to raiding operations, who did not ally among themselves (until the seventeenth century, when the Manchus linked together Mongol tribes and Chinese armies), and who never developed plans and programs aimed at seizing, occupying, and administering Ming territory—until, again, the Manchus did so. It helped, too, that along the two thousand miles of ocean frontier the various pirates, Chinese and Japanese, plus Portuguese, Spanish, and Dutch interlopers, could create much harm but likewise never posed an existential threat aimed at conquest and rule. (The Spanish thought it might be possible to conquer China, but Philip II was not interested, and they never attempted it. Hideyoshi attempted it, but got no farther than Korea. Tamerlane tried it too, but never got beyond Otrar. China was just too far away.) So for 276 years the Ming survived because no outside force seriously challenged it.

The likeliest source of an internal challenge was an angry or ambitious prince. One of them, Zhu Di, Prince of Yan, indeed overthrew the reigning emperor in 1402. But later attempts, as in 1426 and 1519, failed miserably.

But that is not enough to explain Ming China's durability. There were other possible internal sources besides princes to bring down the system.

A combination of lower-class outlaws and rebels and high civilian elites had founded the Ming in the first place. Couldn't that conjunction happen again? Yes, but not until the 1630s and '40s, and then it would almost certainly have failed had it not coincided with Manchu invasion from outside. What of a coup in Beijing? Physical invasions of the Forbidden City by coup-plotters did happen, as noted in the previous chapter. Officials seized control of the enthronement of new emperors on several occasions too. The years 1449, 1457, 1460, 1521, 1615, and 1620 saw such affairs. High civilian, military, and eunuch elites could have conspired to put an end to the dynasty at almost any time, but they never did. Nor was there ever an attempt to split the country by way of secession. In 1402, panicked officials in Nanjing thought of ceding north China to the Prince of Yan; in 1449, panicked officials in Beijing thought about fleeing south and ceding north China to Esen. In 1644, Chongzhen considered, but rejected, the idea of ceding north China to the Manchus. Officials in the provinces never made the slightest move to create independent regimes, even though there were precedents for that deep in China's past. It was not, therefore, sheer force that kept the system together and of a piece; there surely was some sort of national consensus about appropriate and legitimate power relations at work as well.

The Ming emperors, even the bizarre and poorly performing ones, must share some of the credit for the stability and continuity of the system. All edicts and directives emanating from the Forbidden City, even those believed to be forged by eunuchs or those co-signed by palace eunuch Wei Zhongxian, could be protested but in the end they had to be respected and obeyed. It's hard to say why that was, but a cosmic response would be that the roles of emperor and father were conflated in people's minds as absolutely solid objects in nature's unchallengeable hierarchy. It was good to remonstrate with an erring parent or emperor. Those who sent up remonstrances against emperors often adopted the righteous tone of a family junior chiding a senior who was involved in some wrongdoing. Disobedience was, however, a heinous crime of the first order. Widespread agreement on this point was no doubt one of the factors that held the realm together for so long. It seems that for long stretches it did not matter whether the emperor were a good one or not. All the system asked of him was that he should make decisions.

Beyond those considerations, an explanation of Ming longevity demands some understanding of the way the system was constructed, starting from the time of the founder, Ming Taizu. (Some of his institutional engineering has been discussed earlier.) It was he who was advised to separate out the three big components of rule: military, civil, and palace eunuch. Taking his own counsel later, Taizu added a fourth component—his own sons enfeoffed as frontier princes with real though circumscribed military and civil powers of their own. But his fourth son Yongle, who seized power in 1402, permanently took away all princely guards units, so that while the House of Zhu mushroomed in size to many tens of thousands over the course of the Ming, the princes' existence was parasitical, contributing nothing to Ming governance or security—and little to culture, save the occasional playwright or pioneer in acoustics.

As for the other three groups, their fortunes shifted over time. As in the United States, where the White House, Congress, and the courts have seen their relative authority and prestige wax and wane as public opinion and the electoral process have dictated, so too, as the Ming years unfolded, did circumstances and imperial preference allow first one, then another of the three groups of state servitors to rise and fall, and rise and fall again, with respect to the others. That we have seen in the previous chapter.

The founder did much to establish the fundamental features of the system. An eager searcher for advice early in his career, after 1368 Taizu became more and more his own chief counsel. For all his quickness to anger and his cruelty, he was an experimenter. When one institutional experiment didn't work for him, he was always ready to scrap it and try something else. At first, he placed his military commanders at the top of the hierarchy of favored groups. He gave them ritual precedence over civil officials. He rewarded sixty-six of them with feudal-style titles, generous emoluments, and hereditary privileges. His daughters were all married to his generals or their sons. They had won the empire for him, and they were all originally outlaws like himself from the Huai River region of central China. But by the time of his death in 1398, he had destroyed all but eight. All were charged with treason. In 1393, General Lan Yu was accused of planning to assassinate Taizu. The Embroidered-Uniform Guard interrogated hundreds of witnesses and suspected participants under torture. Every one of them testified positively to the assassination charge. Their statements were published. By his own reckoning, Taizu executed fifteen thousand military officers plus relatives and associates for their involvement in the plot. A small military nobility did survive, but it never posed even the faintest threat to the throne for the remainder of the Ming.

Well before this bloodletting, the founder had taken steps to subject the entire military command structure to radical organizational shredding. In

1380 he split the originally unitary Chief Military Commission into five, all headquartered at the capital, with some supervisory control over Regional Military Commissions in the provinces. This move of course reduced the likelihood that any generalissimo could get power and resources enough to try to stage a coup. On top of that, military administration was in part shared out to the Ministry of War. Officer appointments, communications, maintenance, equipment, and strategic planning were the responsibility of the civilian ministry. The military conducted training and field command only. But not entirely, because as the years progressed, emperors more and more assigned eunuchs and civil officials to supervisory roles on the battlefields. And except along the frontiers, such as in Manchuria, military units did not control their own land or supply, which was a responsibility of the civil bureaucracy. This pattern of overlapping and divided powers was an important contributing factor to Ming durability over the long term.[1]

Crucial participants in the power structure of Ming China were the eunuchs. Taizu made a lot of noise about the need to keep their numbers low, their literacy minimal, their caste despised, and their ability to interfere in the processes of government nil. They were simply palace servants and menials, after all. But Taizu violated his own rules, and his successors likewise found eunuchs far too useful as aides in governance to restrict them in the ways the founder had insisted upon. So in 1429 the Xuande emperor set up a palace school to train eunuchs so that they might serve as personal secretaries. That arrangement continued to the end of the Ming. The number of eunuchs living and working inside the palace precincts swelled to perhaps ten or twelve thousand by late Ming, by far the majority involved in housekeeping chores and technical support services of many kinds. Many thousands more unemployed eunuchs formed street gangs in Beijing.

Insofar as they were involved in governing, the eunuch system of offices resembled the system developed in the military and civilian branches—no one in complete charge and organizational transparency, such that emperors had no difficulty punishing and executing any eunuchs that displeased them, including those attached to the Directorate of Ceremonial, the highest of the many eunuch offices. Imperial blessing allowed the occasional eunuch to rise to great power—Wang Zhen, Liu Jin, and Wei Zhongxian especially. Because our sources of information about the eunuchs tend to be spotty and anecdotal, our ignorance about them is substantial. They did have factions, and often they did form ties to this and that network or faction in the civil bureaucracy, that much is clear.

The eunuch offices that were related to governance tended to parallel those assigned the military and the regular bureaucracy. This was one way for the emperors to insert checks and controls into those sectors. For example, there was a Seals Office staffed by regular civil officials and charged with monitoring a large array of imperial seals, the stamps that validated edicts. But there was also a eunuch-run Directorate of Palace Seals, charged with the very same task. There was the palace security service known as the Embroidered-Uniform Guard, staffed by non-eunuchs, and a eunuch-run Eastern Depot, and for a while also a Western Depot, which performed many of the same duties. Most important, there were the Grand Secretariat and the Office of Transmission, charged with the delivery and distribution of documents to and from the emperor, and the scrutiny, discussion, and advice on each memorial coming in and each edict going out. But the Directorate of Ceremonial performed these same duties. Cooperation vied with rivalry as the eunuch agencies and the organs of civil government conducted their overlapping duties day to day. Eunuch commanders were interdigitated with civil officials in leadership roles in many of Ming China's big military operations. Eunuchs such as Cao Jixiang were often put in charge of artillery units. The famous Ming flotillas of 1405–1433 were under the command of Zheng He, a Muslim eunuch from the interior province of Yunnan. Indeed, eunuchs like Isiha were always available to head special high-level missions of any kind, foreign or domestic.[2]

Eunuchs had a part, occasionally and for short periods a dominating part, in governing (notably Wang Zhen, 1446–1449; Liu Jin, 1505–1510, and Wei Zhongxian, 1624–1627). The place of military men was much more subdued. No general or titled military grandee ever achieved more than the Mu family in Yunnan or the Li family in Manchuria, but they were quiet regional actors who shared power with civil and other military officials and never posed threats of any sort. With some exceptions, military officers as a group suffered prejudicial discrimination. Yet they provided regular marriage partners for the Ming imperial house. Emperors such as Chenghua, Zhengde, and Wanli made special efforts to enhance their standing; and civil officials helped design the system of military examinations that from 1464 tested martial arts skills plus knowledge of the military classics, paralleling the provincial and metropolitan civil service examinations and aimed at the younger sons of military families who were not in line to inherit their fathers' ranks. Academically talented sons of military families were also encouraged to try the civil service exams. Many of them succeeded. Unquestionably just the sheer size of Ming China's military arm, coupled with its political passivity, helps explain how the dynasty could last so long. But one has to turn to civil bureaucracy and ask if it were not perhaps the main key to the endurance of the Ming, and if so, how.

There are two ways of looking at this question. One is to probe the internal ordering of Ming bureaucracy. How was it possible to ensure that bureaucracy did what it was supposed to do, that each bureau and each official functioned as intended, and that the right men were trained, selected, posted, and evaluated? Given the size of the bureaucracy, in the twenty thousand range in middle and late Ming times, that was no small task. The other avenue of approach is to assess the quality of the contributions the officials made to the success of the system. This is an impossibly big job, but if it cannot be answered in any definitive way, it can be approached, because the officials took pride in the work they did and, from early Ming to late, left behind a huge archive of documents, letters, comments, and other memorabilia relating to their time in government. The same cannot be said of the eunuchs or military officers, so one needs to be on guard against overstating the bureaucracy's case.

As to the machinery of Ming civil government, it will be convenient for the moment to consider it as a still-life painting, without a time dimension.

One can start with recruitment, the point where bureaucracy touched, affected, and seized the attention of a million or two men and their families at any one time, second only to taxation in the sheer number of people and families that it reached. Taxation was not much welcomed, but bureaucratic recruitment held out to a large proportion of the boys and young men of China the chance at achieving a pinnacle of fame, influence, social prestige, and wealth that no other calling could even begin to rival. (Maritime entrepreneurs in Fujian province successfully funneled their huge profits from smuggling into funding education and examination success for their young men.)

Early Ming government provided the institutional groundwork for the ladder. Taizu set up a national system of schools—eventually one school for each of the 114 prefectures, 193 subprefectures, and 1,138 counties of the realm. Each was provided with one or two paid instructors who actually taught students early in the Ming, but as education more and more fell to private tutors and academies, these functionaries evolved into directors of testing and monitoring only. The basic curriculum of study was established by the Yongle emperor early in the fifteenth century: the Confucian Four Books and Five Classics as annotated by Zhu Xi (1130–1200) and his school of Neo-Confucians, plus study guides and a range of other texts relating to morality and history. Government provided these texts for free early on, but new editions from private printers tended to supplant them as time went on. Student stipends were on offer as well. Nationwide, boys reaching the age of fifteen were tested for admission into the ranks of the *shengyuan* (licentiates; government Confucian students). They were retested many times over to ensure their commitment to study and competence in it. The size of the *shengyuan* population can only be estimated, but it expanded over time, and by late Ming it reached a half million or more. The size of the pool of those who hoped to become *shengyuan* must have been many times bigger.

That any given *shengyuan* would fail to make it through the triennial exams held in his provincial capital (the *juren* degree) and the metropolitan and palace exams held in Beijing the following year (the *jinshi* degree) was a near certainty. Many sat the grueling exams many times over and never passed, due to the rigid quotas: 25 to 130 at the provincial level, depending on the province's population size, and 300 or so at the national. From beginning to end, the Ming examiners (regular members of the bureaucracy appointed to ad hoc committees for the purpose) passed 73,150 *juren* and 24,450 *jinshi*. The failure rates were horrendous and did engender bitterness. Success was sweet, and successful *jinshi* often remembered every detail of the upward ascent; Zhang Ning remembered every twist and turn in his experience of the system over the years 1447 to 1454. Examiners had vivid memories too; the future grand secretary Yan Song later recalled every moment of his experience as an associate reader of the metropolitan exams in 1517. The complaints of failed examinees were legion throughout the Ming: sometimes they blamed an unkind fate or, more often, bias or arbitrary grading by the examiners. But one examiner, Ni Yue (1444–1501), stated in retort that many exam responses made no sense, or were badly expressed, or were a mixture of good and bad parts, like the potpourri of wild and garden vegetables a beggar might be offered at a farmhouse door, little of it palatable.

Almost all *jinshi* could expect an immediate appointment to some office, the importance of the office depending on one's rank order (1–300) on the palace exam. Men holding only the *juren* degree had a long wait for a low post.

There were other and less desirable ways to get a position. A *shengyuan* on a long waiting list, or more rapidly by purchase, could become a National University student in Nanjing or Beijing and, after another long wait, get a very low appointment or an assignment as a local government Confucian teacher. Some government clerks could be accepted into the very lowest ranks in the regular bureaucracy, but there they would remain for the rest of their careers, an inferior and despised caste. (The Chief Grand Secretary Xu Jie's father had gone this route, and he made sure his son did not follow his example.)

The exam system, generation after generation, created a huge log of provincial graduates and licentiates, without posts or any realistic hope of ever getting one. Yet they were not fodder for revolution. They enjoyed fiscal exemptions. They became an educated local elite, a very important social and cultural stratum, whose place in the larger picture of Ming China will be taken up in the next chapter. While provincial quotas minimized regional bias in the awarding of degrees, it was nevertheless true that a relatively small number of affluent counties provided disproportionate advantages to its native sons: half of all graduates came from 146 counties, 13 percent of the total number of counties. These counties lay along the coast of Fujian, along the Gan River valley of Jiangxi, and in the lower Yangzi region of the southern metropolitan province and Zhejiang.

The Ming examination system seems to have been a mechanism that made the regime durable by contributing in so many ways to its success. The best and the brightest youths that the people of China had to offer all went into Ming official service, when there were many other things they might have done. This all came at a price, however. As Lynn Struve has put it, the exam system fostered "the sociopolitical hypocrisy, the intellectual duplicity, dishonesty, constriction and conformity, the moral corruption, class dominance, personal suffering, and the misdirection of human and material resources." That, she states, "abetted autocratic governance, worked against pluralism in thought and society, and inhibited the development of an educational regime that would have better served the people and the economy at large." Indeed so. Yet the opposite was also true: the exam system sustained the system because year after year it captured the hopes, dreams, and ideals of China's young and potentially most capable talents.[3]

The machinery of Ming civil government seems at first glance to have been a simple and streamlined affair, heavily centralized and easily captured in an organizational chart. At the top of the chart sat the emperor, commanding the central bureaucracy in Beijing; the central bureaucracy had charge of the officials in the thirteen provinces and two metropolitan regions (Bei Zhili, centered on Beijing, and Nan Zhili, centered on Nanjing); the provincial officials supervised the prefectures and subprefectures, which in turn controlled all the counties at the bottom of the system, blanketing the whole territory of Ming China. This is technically called a "nested hierarchy," with each lower-level unit tucked inside some higher unit until the emperor is reached, sitting solo atop it all. The reality was rather more complicated.

First, after 1380 central bureaucracy had no prime minister at its head. No one person could by law control it or speak for it. The Grand Secretariat as the highest bureaucratic unit was an advisory board, not an executive organ. The chief grand secretaries who dominated affairs through much of the sixteenth century achieved their sway by cultivating close personal relationships with the emperor and his leading eunuchs, and by building up a personal machine of devotees, supporters, and hangers-on in the civil bureaucracy. After Zhang Juzheng's death in 1582, no one was able to rise to that level again. Power at the top of the civil bureaucracy remained effectively fragmented. It was not easy for grand secretaries to accrue personal power, because they were for the most part men who had finished at or near the top of the rank-order list in the metropolitan examinations and had been given editorial tasks in the Hanlin Academy, and thus lacked administrative experience and close working ties with the regular bureaucrats.

Secondly, the actual executive organs of the civil government were divided functionally, but no one organ dominated its own main function. None of the Six Ministries (Personnel, Revenue, Rites, War, Justice, and Works) could fully control its respective sphere of competence. For example, Personnel did not have exclusive charge of all matters relating to personnel; the Ministry of Justice shared the review and adjudication of appeals and other cases with the Censorate and the Court of Judicial Review. Many other examples can be adduced.

Third, further complicating the picture, but contributing to the sustainability of the system, were the controls imposed upon document flow. Two offices were involved: the Office of Transmission and six Offices of Scrutiny. The latter, assigned to each of the Six Ministries, staffed usually by promising young holders of the *jinshi* degree, could protest and place holds on both memorials coming up to the emperor, as well as inappropriate rescripts and edicts coming down. They could also join with the Censorate in voicing opinions on current policy and in remonstrating against the emperor. These Supervising Secretaries, together with the Censors, were jointly known as *yanguan* ("speaking officials") or *kedao*. As such, they commanded great celebrity (and at times provoked controversy, anger, and bitterness) as self-styled guardians of the moral and political health of the realm. They were also vulnerable to factionalism.

The six Offices of Scrutiny and their forty (later downsized to thirty-two) officials were not organized into any kind of clear hierarchy. The Censorate had something approaching a hierarchy—two censors-in-chief headed a group of 123 officials, plus 168 clerks and several hundred trainee-observers. Censorial appointments were, however, the prerogative of the emperor, not the censors-in-chief. The censors wielded a big stick over the civil bureaucracy because they were empowered to monitor the activities of everyone in it and issue impeachments whenever they saw fit. Carefully selected, the censors, like the supervising secretaries, were younger men for the most part, and their bureaucratic ranking low. But they could look forward to future promotions to higher positions. If one searches for sources of energy in a system that was susceptible to sclerosis, the *kedao* is definitely one of first places to look.

Fourth, there was another feature of the system that contributed to the longevity of the Ming empire, and it involved the Censorate in a different way. The emperor could inject a powerful downward thrust from Beijing into the provinces, regions, and frontiers by way of ad hoc commissions and special appointments, often to the Censorate, bypassing the regular organs assigned to those places. For instance, the regular apparatus of provincial government featured an administration commission (headed by two men), plus a military commission and a surveillance commission. They were loaded with routine work. But it was a noteworthy feature of Ming government, commented upon by foreign observers like Ricci and Semedo, to appoint so-called regional inspectors (*xun'an*) to annual terms in the provinces and on the frontiers, with full power to probe everywhere and issue orders and impeachments. Other censors were often sent out from Beijing on special assignments to check military registers, distribute relief, audit the salt monopoly, monitor and test local *shengyuan* (licentiates), and so on. Above all these in rank were Grand Coordinators (*xunfu*) and Supreme Commanders (*zongdu*), civil officials with nominal censorial appointments who acted like super governors in the provinces and on the frontiers, usually with military campaign responsibilities. These appointees injected great energy into an otherwise very stiff bureaucratic structure.

Lastly, Ming China's civil bureaucracy spent a great deal of time and effort on performance evaluations for every one of its members. The highest-ranking officials, grand secretaries for example, had to send up periodic self-evaluations to the emperor, but everyone else was rated every three years by his superiors, and then either promoted, kept in the same office, or demoted. All terms lapsed after nine years, when a shift of office would have to be made. The Censorate vetted these ratings, and then sent them to the Ministry of Personnel for appropriate action. There were yet other ratings. There was the so-called "outer evaluation." Provincial and prefectural officials rated all local officials and sent these every three years to Beijing for joint review by the Censorate and the Ministry of Personnel. There was also the "capital evaluation" every five to nine years, for officials based in Beijing. There were impromptu evaluations conducted by censors or regional inspectors. And then anyone could be impeached at any time, or promoted at any time; there was no need to wait for the periodic reviews. The surprise is that, as with the examination system, the corruption of the evaluations process, through bribery or partisan activity, though occasionally suspected, seems usually to have been negligible. Partisanship was usually expressed through ad hoc impeachments, not the scheduled evaluations.

What does all this imply for Ming longevity? Civil government was not the only large group at the emperor's disposal, nor was it the largest. The military was by far the largest and costliest. But it did things eunuchs, soldiers, or Embroidered-Uniform Guardsmen (the imperial police) could not: rule the people at large, adjudicate their disputes, and collect most of the taxes. Civil government embodied tensions—between conservatism and a kind of radicalism; between dull and unchanging foundational scaffolding and ad hoc and innovative overlays; between long-established lethargy and new sources of energy. Emperors through Xuande provided that energy; then at various times eunuchs, grand secretaries, *kedao*, and various *xunfu* and *zongdu* stepped in. Wang Yangming, the inspirational leader of a new moral-philosophical movement in Confucianism, while very busy as a *xunfu* in far-off Jiangxi province in the early sixteenth century, was able to attract students and other intellectuals and exert influences that were truly national in scope, and indeed, reinvigorate the whole ethos of officialdom.

Civil bureaucracy was a precarious, even dangerous employer to serve, but it provided a national stage that everyone watched closely, where important things could be said and done, where copious written records were kept, where history was being created and compiled, where the people's lives could be protected and improved, where China itself could be made a better place, where reputations and fortunes were made and unmade, where one could immortalize oneself and one's parents and establish a positive legacy for one's children and grandchildren and leave a permanent mark in the annals of the civilization. This kind of literary glory was well beyond the reach of eunuchs and most military men, and few emperors, even, could achieve it. These attractions help explain how, generation after generation, the best talents of the realm could be recruited into state service, despite the low official salaries that were on offer.[4]

⁓

Aside from the energizers just discussed, most of the officials at the center and in the provinces and prefectures worked by the book and carried out routine duties, and spent much of their time on semi-technical tasks and on checking and evaluating subordinates lower down the hierarchy. They seldom dealt with the public head-on. It was in the subprefectures and counties that the real governing of the people took place. Somehow, the regime's ability to stay afloat for so long depended upon the nature of the interface between government and people at those lowest levels.

The Ming founder, Taizu, had lived under Yuan local government, and his experience of it convinced him that the Yuan dynasty had fallen in large part because it did not control official corruption and oppression at the local level. His remedy for the problem underwent several revisions, but none so drastic as that which accompanied the 1380 reorganization of the central and provincial bureaucracies. Convinced that civil bureaucrats at every level were hopelessly venal and treacherous, his decision, in essence, was to remove county magistrates from direct rule altogether. He forbade them to venture any more beyond the confines of their county offices to harass the people they ruled. The work of local government would now devolve to the people themselves to carry out. He organized all the villagers of China into *lijia*, units of 110 taxpaying households led by the ten richest among them. Those leaders would collect the grain taxes and ship that grain at their own expense to Nanjing or whichever distant depot the central authorities might designate. The other main duty of local government, resolving disputes and preserving law and order, was put in hands of groups parallel to the *lijia* called "village elders" (*qisu*). Other local worthies were urged to act as censors, wielding powers of impeachment and arrest against all evildoing officials and clerks.

The founder himself was disappointed with the results of these downward intrusions into local society, and they were mostly allowed to lapse after his death. Then the Yongle emperor's ambitious programs placed so much tax pressure on the *lijia* as to wreck them. Responsibility for the collection and shipment of taxes then fell by default back to the county magistrates and other local officials, each of whom had to develop his own methods to fulfill his quota of taxes. This led to much county-to-county variation across the length and breadth of Ming China. Generally, however, the magistrates froze the household registers so as to allow population increase to have the effect of diluting and thus reducing the tax burden. Also they tried to keep newly opened land off the books for as long as possible.

As the years wore on, this state of affairs evolved into a situation in which the regional inspectors placed heavy pressures on county magistrates to fulfill their annual tax quotas, but left them with much latitude as to how they did it. Magistrates were often young *jinshi* (metropolitan degree-holders) from the middle and lower places on the graduation lists. They enjoyed great discretionary power and were encouraged to make good contacts with the local members of the educated elite, often retired officials; and if they did well, they could look forward to future promotions up the bureaucratic ladder. Undesirable counties along the frontiers, or in poverty-stricken regions of the interior, however, were often assigned to older men with provincial degrees or other inferior credentials. Magistrates could not serve in their home provinces, and their tenures in office tended to shorten over time to the minimum three years, after which the regional inspectors evaluated them. They might end up dismissed, penalized, transferred to more difficult (and lucrative) counties, or promoted up into provincial or central administration.

How all this affected the stability and durability of the whole Ming system is an interesting question. Several positive factors, some unintentional, seem clear. One was that the dynasty was assured year after year of administrators of ability and good quality in most of the richer tax-producing counties of the realm. Another was that, when central authority was no longer so concerned with life at ground level as it had been in Taizu's time, or so knowledgeable about it, possibilities opened for a measure of flexibility and the possibility of piecemeal change in local government. Nothing better exemplifies this than the great shift in the national tax system from taxation in kind and personally performed labor service early on, to a system based solely on silver payments, over the course of the sixteenth century. This so-called single whip reform was not imposed by central fiat. It was initiated at the local level by no one in particular. The center just passively accepted it. The collective power of the local magistrates also ensured that the center was kept ignorant of the true sources of wealth in the realm. The tax burden, even adding in the seventeenth-century tax surcharges, never threatened the realm's ability to pay. Indeed, Ming China was undertaxed. The Qing dynasty later saw fit to continue much of this system unchanged, which must be considered as testimony to its viability.[5]

⌢

What of the quality of Ming government? Was it good government, or bad? A hard question, because it is difficult to poll the people of Ming China who were subject to it to find out. Surrogate methods have to be tried. To be sure Ming government was flawed in many ways, but what governing system isn't? The Ming has long lain under a cloud of opprobrium for such things as its appalling custom of court flogging, its routine use of judicial torture, its grossly swollen corps of palace eunuchs (or the recourse to eunuchs at all), its huge and parasitic class of imperial clansmen, its roster of low-grade emperors. To that one might add routinized corruption and the increasingly dysfunctional and eventually lethal factionalism that plagued its central administration, especially during its last half-century. There is no hiding the fact that there was a crazed and bloody edge to Ming politics. But that is not the whole story. Many generations of men—civil officials, military men, and, yes, eunuchs—gave the dynasty good and conscientious service, even though they may also have been partisans, may have been ambitious and self-interested, and may have even been conventionally corrupt.

The evidence, albeit indirect, lies in the unprecedented quantity of publication about contemporary administration that came out in Ming times, especially in the sixteenth and seventeenth centuries: administrative handbooks (such as advice books for local magistrates); institutional guidebooks to many of the different component parts of Ming government; big collections of the biographies of noted officials; personal memoirs; and collections of state papers relating to a wide range of problems and issues that arose during the course of the dynasty. The document collections make it clear that many people devoted much thought and effort over a long period of time to the whole range of concrete challenges and difficulties of ruling China. The cumulative result of such efforts could only have been to help prolong the system.

It is relevant to the issue of quality in Ming administration that governance had from early on an intellectual and scholarly dimension that surely lifted it from the humdrum and encouraged people to think hard about it. A major contribution in this direction was the awkwardly named *Daxue yanyi bu* ("Supplement to the Extended Meaning of the Great Learning"), a thick guide to governance presented to the Hongzhi emperor by the quarrelsome Vice Minister of Rites Qiu Jun in 1487, and printed for general circulation in 1488. This work, widely read, and first in a long series of administrative studies published during the Ming, focused attention on the entire scope of what government should do and how it should do it. Its twelve sections and 119 subsections covered the imperial court; the civil bureaucracy; fiscal matters; the state ritual program; education; policing and communications; judicial administration; military affairs; border defense and foreign relations; and the ideological and spiritual relevance of Cheng-Zhu Neo-Confucianism to all of the above. (Some of Qiu's ideas were ahead of their time: he favored sea transportation; the liberalization of foreign trade; and the replacement of labor services by a tax in silver, developments which had to wait a century for their fulfillment.) Later work on governance tended to be based more on gathered sources reproduced verbatim, less on essay-style exposition.[6]

An outstanding example of such a collection is the *Huang Ming jingshi wenbian* ("Compendium of Ming Documents on Ordering the World"), published in 1638. Note the late date. Unease and concern about the dynasty's future prompted a romantic poet and newly minted metropolitan degree-holder, Chen Zilong (1608–1647), and two comrades, members of the Restoration Society (discussed further in the next chapter), to undertake and complete the project in about six months. Their aim was to transcend the ongoing partisan gridlock and show it was possible for officials to identify and solve problems in a realistic way, because officials had done just that over the whole earlier span of the dynasty's history. The work contains in roughly chronological order items from the writings, most of it already published but scattered over many books, of 421 officials, mostly mid- to upper-level. It includes personal letters that discuss administrative problems; memos and directives sent from one official to another relating to field operations; inscriptions for cutting into stone, describing the completion of large public works projects—seawalls, bridges, river improvements, granaries, office buildings, ferries, Great Wall sections and other defense works, and so on. There are discussions and proposals put forth at top-level court conferences. Most of the documents are memorials and reports to the throne, describing problems in great detail and suggesting remedies, or asking for authorization to do certain things. Chen Zilong gave special attention in his selections to frontier troubles, the northern frontier especially, and also to Yellow River conservancy; military rosters, organization, supply, deployment, weaponry, and defense works; famines; banditry; the imperial clan—plus a vast miscellany of other matters, all of it very practical, with little coverage at all of *kedao* impeachments, ideological disputes, or partisan broadsides.

To get a concrete glimpse of what all this can tell us at this distance in time about the quality of Ming governance, it might help to turn, pretty much at random (many other illustrative picks might be made) to the thirty-nine documents written by Tu Zemin, by now a long-forgotten mid-level official who was active in the later phases of the eventually successful Ming suppression of the Wokou (Sino-Japanese piracy) on the coasts of Fujian and Guangdong provinces in the late 1560s. No Ming source has a biography or epitaph for Tu. More prominent than he in the coastal actions were Hu Zongxian and the highly literate military men Qi Jiguang and Yu Dayou, with detailed life histories and published works of their own available. But Tu Zemin made important contributions to the hard work of suppressing the piracy. A metropolitan degree holder from Sichuan province, deep in the interior, Tu held a dual position as Grand Coordinator of Fujian province and concurrent military censor-in-chief. His polite letters to colleagues and curt directives to military commanders show he had a close hand in devising strategy; deploying local, extra-provincial, and non-Chinese troops; building boats of various types; figuring out what to do with surrendered pirates; begging Fujian provincial elites to assist with supply; issuing guidelines on the acquisition and use of cannon and fowling pieces; issuing rewards; and urging that locals be directed to poison the food supplies they were sending to pirates offshore. That and more Tu elaborated in great detail, and the *Huang Ming jingshi wenbian* editors alertly provide interlinear notes and topical rubrics to help readers follow what was afoot. (Tu Zemin was also one official voice in favor of easing the standing ban on foreign trade, a measure taken in 1567 after the Jiajing emperor's death. The joint efforts of Tu and his colleagues brought about the destruction of pirates Wu Ping and Zeng Yiben and their followers in 1569. Pirate Lin Daoqian [known to Westerners as Lim Dao Kiam or Lintoquian] escaped with five thousand well-armed men and some hundred ships, including six big ones, and began a new career in Southeast Asia. But Tu's file shows that the Ming faced problems of scale and complexity, and solved them or at least palliated them, thanks to the cooperation of many different civil officials and military officers.)[7]

Chen Zilong's compilation was a private undertaking. There is another big (and quasi-official) late Ming compilation that can be brought to the discussion of the dynasty's administration. This one is the *Guochao xianzheng lu*, edited by Jiao Hong (1541–1620), and printed in 1616. This began as an officially sponsored project undertaken by the Hanlin Academy in Beijing, and was intended as part of a larger project of compiling materials for a future general history of the Ming. However, the project's chief, Grand Secretary Chen Yubi, died in 1597, and work stopped. So Jiao Hong continued it on his own as a private citizen in Nanjing. This work reprints verbatim epitaphs and other biographical accounts of no fewer than 3,071 men who served as officials from the founding of the Ming down to around 1600. Of course, this is but a small and probably unrepresentative fraction of all those who served during the first two Ming centuries. Those included are listed under which-ever office was the highest they achieved during their careers. The compiler includes 1,651 central officials who achieved their highest offices in Beijing; 523 who ended up serving in the secondary capital of Nanjing; and 897 whose careers ended in one of the thirteen provinces and two metropolitan regions. Many biographies are long, and many touch but little on the final office achieved, which might occupy but a short period in the context of a much longer career.

Two studies, done some years ago, draw on much larger databases to offer some conclusions about the quality of Ming governance. One considers all the top ministry officials from 1380 to 1644 and, assuming that length of tenure correlates with dynastic stability, which it may, finds early instability yielding to high stability in the Yongle era (1402–1424), then a long down-ward slide featuring shortening tenures, ending in another bout of instability in the 1620–1644 era. A later study uses data on 23,000 central, provincial, and local officials to come to a fairly similar conclusion. What the *Guochao xianzheng lu* with its many career stories, each one different, but most of them with a positive or at least neutral spin, can tell us is something about the fine grain of real administrative experience. Any of the biographies can serve as a window of sorts on the question of quality. Leafing through the *Guochao xianzheng lu* and pulling out stories more or less at random from the biographies and epitaphs of officials who occupied (1) local, (2) central, and (3) regional positions yields these three: Zheng Shunchen (1515–1592) at the local level, Lu Guangzu (1521–1597) mainly at the central, and Ma Lu (1477–1544) at the regional. Let us see where their stories take us.[8]

Zheng Shunchen wrote a long autobiography covering his career in great detail. He wrote it for his descendants, but obviously he expected a wider readership, and Jiao Hong included it in the section devoted to officials who achieved their highest posts in Guangxi province in the far south.

Zheng presents himself as earnest, smart, hardworking, brave, conscien-tious, compassionate, generous to a fault, but a hero who was ill starred. In a different age, his life could have been made into a television miniseries. He was born into what appears to have been a rich family of good ancestry living in Shangyu County in Zhejiang province. His father, posted in 1534 to Suiqi county (in Guangdong province, two hundred miles southeast of Canton) as a police officer, somehow got put in charge of building a seawall, a job he took seriously, even coming out to the work site with basket and shovel himself to help. The job was done in eight months. Fifty years later it was still in service, and locals named it the Zheng Dike in his honor. That was a good example for his son. But reading about Fan Zhongyan, the famous eleventh-century statesman, also inspired young Zheng. Fan's charitable works so impressed him that he tried always to emulate them in his own life and career. Zheng was ever ready to help people he found in dire poverty or unfairly treated by the courts.

After a long hard struggle and many setbacks, Zheng passed his provincial exams in 1546 and finally won his metropolitan (*jinshi*) degree in 1556. Several of the intervening years he spent in Xinghua prefecture in Fujian province where a friend who was a magistrate appointed him a teacher to the local government students. There he interceded effectively on behalf of a poor couple whose only son, wrongly accused, was due to be executed. A relative offered Zheng a reward for that: the son's beautiful young wife! Zheng of course declined the offer.

Armed with the *jinshi* degree, Zheng was appointed magistrate of Shexian in present-day southern Anhui province, a very demanding post, not suitable for a young man to try to cope with, but Zheng was by this time forty-one. Immediately a mountain of pending litigation faced him, and a higher central official was demanding an immediate delivery of construction timber. Without providing details, Zheng wrote that he dealt with all this fairly and conscientiously. Then a fire that started in the south of the county seat destroyed some twenty homes and threatened the seat itself. Zheng prayed to Heaven, offering his own family and himself as sacrifices. Heaven heard. The wind shifted, and Shexian was saved. Zheng took great interest in the county school students, and out of his own pocket bought two hundred *mou* of fields to support needy students and honest clerks. At the end of three years he received a top rating. On his departure for Beijing, the Shexian people turned out in great number, burning incense and weeping, some accompanying him for many miles along the way. Three shrines commemorating his service were built in his honor.

In Beijing, a large file of positive censorial evaluations and recommendations had been compiled in his behalf. Zheng could surely look forward to a significant promotion. But upon arrival in the capital, Zheng discovered to his dismay that to win a promotion, he would have to sign on to Chief Grand Secretary Yan Song's patronage machine, and that of course he refused to do.

We will skim rapidly over Zheng's next few assignments (which he does cover in detail): Bureau Secretary in the Ministry of Works in Nanjing; then in effect demoted (at the behest of Yan Song's son) to Vice Prefect of Deng-zhou prefecture in Henan; then Magistrate of Tongzhou subprefecture east of Beijing; then (in 1569) Vice Prefect of Yuanzhou in Jiangxi. There he found the old residence of Yan Song, who had died in disgrace in 1565, a total ruin. "Where is all that power and glory today?" he wondered.

After less than a year in Yuanzhou, Zheng received his final office: Prefect of Liuzhoufu, located roughly in the center of Guangxi province in far south China, and not by any means a desirable posting. "Though enclosed within the bounds of our civilization and jurisdiction," wrote Zheng, "most of the territory is occupied by Yao and Zhuang people. Outside the prefectural city there are only three villages that [Chinese] commoners live in." On arrival, Zheng found an army of a hundred thousand "wolf troops" (non-Chinese fighters) camped just outside the city. They were part of a big military operation being mounted against other non-Chinese who had rebelled in Gutian (near present-day Nanning, some hundred miles to the south). Zheng repaired the Liuzhou city walls to keep it safe. He tried to rein in the wolf troops, who were undisciplined and addicted to rape and plunder. The other officials were doing nothing to stop them, for fear of provoking a mutiny. Zheng arranged with the military intendant to seize four of their leaders and hang them publicly without revealing their names or their crimes. That tactic put so much doubt into the fighters' minds that they stopped marauding. Another military intendant arrested several hundred fighters and scheduled them all for execution; but on reviewing their cases, Zheng took pity on sixty young ones, so on his own authority he released them and replaced them with sixty older men. He was just about to turn to some longer-term projects, education and tax reform and the like, when he was given a bad evaluation and in 1571 was forced to retire. A colleague who long ago had some reason for resenting Zheng denounced him to a Beijing censor who had ties to Chief Grand Secretary Zhang Juzheng, whose star was on the rise at the time. So Zheng's career ended badly.

"That was my fate," he concluded. "What could I have done about it? I was just an ordinary fellow who grounded his career in loyalty and liberality, whose every thought during twenty years of official service was to cherish the people and do nothing that was not in the public interest. I never indulged in trickery or falsity, nor did I ever knock at the gates of the high and mighty."

What can Zheng Shunchen's story tell us about the quality of Ming bureaucracy? Supposing his autobiography to be truthful, perhaps few officials combined his philanthropy, honesty, sincerity, perseverance, and initiative. Perhaps many shared a few of those traits. He was a small cog in a big machine, but he touched many lives and must have given thousands of common people cause to think well of Ming government. What the ethnic minorities in Guangxi might have thought about him is not recorded.[9]

⌒

Lu Guangzu (1521–1597) had a very different and more successful career than did Zheng. Like his contemporary, however, he came from a good Zhejiang family of learning and pedigree, Pinghu county in his case. Like Zheng, he was an idealistic youth inspired by Fan Zhongyan, in his case by Fan's advice to "take the realm as one's personal responsibility." He passed his *jinshi* degree in 1547 at the fairly young age of twenty-six, and in 1548 was given his first appointment as magistrate of Xunxian (also pronounced Junxian), a county about 250 miles south of Beijing. This was a challenge for a new and young appointee, because it lay on a major highway and many of its inhabitants had fled. We are told he reduced the tax and service burden by reducing the number of fiscal villages (*li*) from fifty to forty. Then he built a wall around the county seat for protection against marauders, with whom some of the local people surreptitiously sympathized. Young civil official though he was, Lu raised and trained a defense militia that became very loyal to him, and forced a big outlaw band that was causing destruction everywhere to give Xunxian a wide berth. He also fought off fierce pressure from higher officials and succeeded in relieving his people of a requirement to provide forced labor for Great Wall rebuilding projects. He urged instead that the people of south China should be taxed for this, and that the proceeds should be used to hire his people for the task. He also kept the local Ming princes from seizing land and encroaching upon the salt monopoly. But his most attention-getting act was his judicious handling of a case involving a local rich man and provocative litterateur of disagreeable temper by the name of Lu Nan (no relation), and playing an important role in getting him released from prison in Beijing, where he had been held for some time on charges of murder. Why defend such a person? "All I can tell is whether he's guilty or not," Lu explained. "I don't care if he's rich or poor." From that, reportedly, Lu came to be noted and widely consulted for his legal judgment.

His term at Xunxian completed, Lu was qualified for rapid upward promotion to a post in Beijing, but because he was distantly related to Lu Bing (1510–1560), the controversial commander of the emperor's palace police, the Embroidered-Uniform Guard, he prudently decided to avoid Beijing and seek a post in Nanjing instead. So in 1552 he was made Secretary of the Bureau of Sacrifices in that secondary capital. That was light duty.

The patronage of senior officials helped Lu with his career. Eventually Minister of Personnel Yan Na (1511–1584) brought him back to Beijing, where because of his talent and good judgment, his patron gave him in effect free rein to set policy for the ministry. This was in 1563–1565, toward the end of the Jiajing period. Lu collaborated with Chief Grand Secretary Xu Jie (1503–1583) in identifying and recalling to Beijing a number of renowned senior officials who had long been in political exile; and beyond that, he saw to it that some worthy and capable men who lacked examination degrees were rewarded and promoted to higher office. These and some other steps he took to break "stale habits" and effect refreshing reform in personnel management. But while many welcomed his acts, he also provoked heated opposition. Denounced by a censor for exceeding his station and wrongfully exercising power, he was removed from the official registry and lived at home in Pinghu for the next six years, technically as a commoner, without fiscal privileges.

In Pinghu, he joined his father in donating money and fields to support local charity. Though out of office and therefore power, he volunteered to help when in 1570–1572 Chief Grand Secretary Xu Jie was forced into retirement and his gigantic estates in Huating county, not far from Pinghu, came near to being confiscated.

Lu Guangzu did not share Zheng Shunchen's aversion to accepting patronage. It seems that the powerful Chief Grand Secretary Zhang Juzheng, who prized talent, was responsible for restoring Lu to the official registry and recalling him to Beijing to serve as Chief Minister of the Court of Judicial Review. But Zhang came under fierce assault from the *kedao* (censors and supervising secretaries) and was unable to protect Lu from the same. Lu resigned and went home again. On Zhang's death in 1582, Lu was recalled and interested himself in northern frontier problems; but a renewed round of censorial attacks sent him bouncing between posts in Beijing and Nanjing and back home again in retirement.

A few years later he was made Nanjing Minister of Personnel, and as such, he joined Geng Dingxiang (1524–1596), Nanjing censor-in-chief, in an indictment of Zhang Jing, one of the more predatory of Wanli's revenue-collecting eunuchs. Despite that, he was made Minister of Justice in Beijing in 1590. There he helped win the release of Li Cai (1520–ca. 1606), a high official and a philosopher as well, under sentence of death for falsifying reports about his role in Ming fighting against the Burmese in Yunnan.

In line with the high turnover rate characteristic of the Wanli era, Lu was made Beijing Minister of Personnel in 1591, a post he held and exercised energetically until he retired for good the next year, when the palace eunuchs and grand secretaries pressured successfully for his dismissal. He died six years later. (The *Huang Ming jingshi wenbian* includes several memorials of his relating to the conduct of personnel evaluations.)

It is related that when Lu was ousted for exceeding his authority back in the 1560s, he met the censor who impeached him, Sun Peiyang (1532–1614), on the main boulevard outside the Imperial City. "I'm just a simple and naïve fellow," said Lu in a calm and friendly way, "yet I'm ousted because of what you charged me with. You went too far when you said I usurped power!" Sun cringed in shame. Later on, as a personnel official, he assisted Sun and several other censors who had earlier attacked him because he valued their talent and did not take their impeachments of him personally.

Unmentioned in his biography in the *Guochao xianzheng lu* is his friendly debate with a Korean envoy in 1566 over the relative merits of Zhu Xi and Wang Yangming, a common topic of dispute at the time. The envoy defended Zhu Xi. Lu defended Wang Yangming.

Lu Guangzu achieved a higher sequence of offices than Zheng Shunchen ever did, but it would be hard to say that Lu's career was any more fulfilling. It was not a good time to serve in high office. After Zhang Juzheng's demise, the Wanli emperor treated civil officials with cold contempt. Terms in office were brief. Posts often went unfilled. The *kedao* overused their powers of impeachment. They continually hounded Lu Guangzu. Yet Lu had a special feel for legal judgment and personnel management, and he tended to get positions that allowed him to exercise his particular talents. If his epitaph is at all truthful, he remained idealistic to the end and used his considerable savoir-faire to help others, and while he early on looked to powerful patrons, he stayed aloof from the bitter partisan rivalries that were creating havoc at the top levels of civil government. Early on, he had been deeply impressed by and helped to protect the great Buddhist intellectual and revivalist Zhenke (1544–1604), and perhaps some of Zhenke's attitudes rubbed off on him. So if the Ming survived for so long, perhaps it was in part because men like Lu Guangzu did make the realm their personal responsibility, and exerted a benign influence in what was otherwise an increasingly dismal state of affairs.[10]

Partisan-inspired malfunction was not just a phenomenon of the Wanli era. The Jiajing era was also infected with it. The career of Ma Lu (1477–1544) was deeply affected by it. Ma, a censorial official from Xinyang (about 125 miles north of present-day Wuhan, in southern Henan province), had a big part in one such episode in 1527.

We have no personal background on Ma Lu, other than his having achieved the *jinshi* degree in 1508, having done well as a county magistrate, and, as Regional Inspector, having deflected a threatened mass crackdown by the Embroidered-Uniform Guard on local officials in 1522.

Then in 1527 there arose the never-solved Li Fuda case, officially the "Great Case." It soon ended in wrecking the career of some forty officials, including Ma Lu's. Li Fuda was not important, nor was his so-called case, yet he somehow touched off a heated battle involving the young Jiajing emperor and the highest military grandee of the time, Marquis Guo Xun (1475–1542). The marquis had been one of Jiajing's staunchest supporters in the Great Rites controversy of 1524.

In 1527, the earnest and hardworking Ma Lu was sent out to Shanxi province as a Regional Inspector. In what at first seemed to be a routine piece of business, Ma arrested and prepared a case against one Li Fuda, a long-sought fugitive, a onetime organizer for the messianic and violent White Lotus society, who had been exiled to a military guards unit on the Great Wall frontier. He escaped, but was found hiding in Luchuan county in Shaanxi province under an assumed name, Zhang Yin. He had somehow gone into business shipping grain to the frontier military. Three sons of his had moved to Beijing, where they got themselves registered as residents under the artisan category. One or more of the sons entered Guo Xun's luxurious Beijing mansion where he (or they) worked alchemy, turning out Daoist elixirs for aphrodisiac or other purposes. The son or sons must have heard of their father's plight and told the marquis about it. The marquis sent a letter to Ma Lu, asking him to drop the case. Surely a bribe was also on offer. Ma Lu not only refused the request; he charged Guo Xun with being a party to treason! There may have been legal grounds for such a charge, but it was a disastrous decision to take politically.

When the case came up to Beijing, the young emperor hastily ordered the arrest and execution of Li Fuda and his sons, the enslavement of his wife and daughters, and the confiscation of all the family's property. Then he had second thoughts. He deferred judgment on Guo Xun. So at that juncture, nineteen Beijing *kedao* jointly impeached Guo Xun, hoping that Jiajing would decide in their favor. Jiajing called in Guo Xun. Guo apologized, but he convinced the emperor that he was really being impeached because of his role in the Great Rites affair.

Meanwhile Li Fuda was transported to Beijing for interrogation by the *fasi* (the Censorate, Grand Court of Revision, and Ministry of Justice acting jointly). The *fasi* confirmed the original charges. Jiajing made them confer again. "We already decided this," complained one official to another. "Why are we discussing it again?" These remarks were overheard, reported to the police, and the offending officials placed under arrest. But the *fasi* stood by its original verdict.

Jiajing responded in fury. All the officials involved were arrested and hustled off to the Decree Prison run by the Embroidered-Uniform Guard. There they were tortured until they confessed to having made false charges. It was now alleged that the man arrested under the name Zhang Yin was indeed Zhang Yin and not Li Fuda. He was pardoned and allowed to go home. The officials were variously exiled in perpetuity to frontier garrisons, or removed from officialdom, or dismissed from office and sent home. The emperor was especially hard on the *kedao*, and exceptionally angry with Ma Lu. He was persuaded, however, not to execute Ma, but rather sentence him and his sons and grandsons to perpetual exile in a garrison in a malarial area of Guangxi province.

As did many other political exiles, Ma taught students, wrote poems, and enjoyed strong drink. He died in exile seventeen years later. (The other purge victims were gradually pardoned; a few returned after a few years to office, others were amnestied when Jiajing produced his first son in 1537, and the rest were restored to grace, in some cases posthumously, at the accession of the Longqing emperor in 1567. Government published its side of the story in the same year that it occurred, 1527.)

Thus the Li Fuda case turned out to be merely a step forward in another matter altogether, a continuing purge of the supporters of the former Chief Grand Secretary Yang Tinghe and all the other bureaucrats who had opposed Jiajing in the Great Rites matter. It throws a harsh and negative light on the quality of Ming governance. It shows that in a determined standoff, the emperor could prevail over a helpless civil bureaucracy, and it demonstrates that emotionalism and factionalism could at times take charge of men's minds at the expense of all else. Nonetheless, Ming government withstood this and many other violent internal eruptions, proof of its resilience and durability in the longer run.[11]

The thrust of this review of Ming governance tends toward the positive: to provide some answers to the question of how the system could have lasted for so long. Undeveloped is the question whether and to what extent government (or misgovernment) might have contributed to the eventual collapse. But collapse is best explained by long-term pathologies. After nearly three centuries of rule, there were quantitative signs that the Ming system was running low on steam. Population had swelled, possibly tripled. Per capita wealth probably failed to keep up and may have declined. Income differences between the rich and the poor may have widened. Rural bondservant revolts were breaking out in several parts of the country. Factional infighting in Beijing became ever more lethal. Worst of all, tax income could not keep pace with military and other expenditures. Military desertions grew in severity. These developments together created a toxic mess that probably lay well beyond the capacity of any preindustrial government to solve. That the Qing dynasty chose to retain so much of the Ming apparatus of rule is strong evidence that the positive aspects of the Ming system of governance outweighed in many respects its defects, and that it cannot be assigned too much of the blame for the Ming downfall.

CHAPTER FOUR

~

Literati

The civil service examination system, endured by so many and successfully negotiated by so few, was unquestionably the central shaping mechanism, in many ways the driving mechanism, behind the formation, generation after generation, of the educated elite of Ming China. All over China, education—whether delivered in private lineage schools, private academies, Buddhist temples, or early in Ming times, in prefectural and county schools—was geared to preparing students to meet the standardized requirements of the examination system. Thus almost every person who ever went to school had at least a rudimentary introduction to the Four Books, the Five Classics, Chinese history, and the fundamentals of Cheng-Zhu Neo-Confucianism.

The longer the Ming lasted, the larger grew the educated class, commonly referred to in the Western literature on China as "literati." The total Ming population may have tripled from an original sixty million or so to nearly two hundred million by the time of its collapse in 1644. The population of licentiates or *shengyuan* (officially registered government Confucian students) did even better. It grew exponentially, from some fifty thousand in 1500 to as many as half a million by the end of the Ming, with millions of others waiting in the wings. From the cadet ranks of the *shengyuan* came officials, and a much larger non-official public of readers, writers, playwrights, and intellectuals of all sorts. All this growth took place on a middle and late Ming wave of commercial prosperity and increasing urbanization. A rather stark and simple world in early Ming evolved into an extraordinarily complex one by late Ming.

⌒

In Yuan and very early Ming, it was not unusual for scholars and teachers to set aside the inherited Cheng-Zhu commentary on the sacred Confucian texts and freelance, making one's own sense of the archaic and often cryptic language of the originals. In 1404, the Yongle emperor made it clear that this kind of intellectual inquiry, which compromised the validity of the officially sanctioned Cheng-Zhu interpretations, would be tolerated no longer, and anyone who engaged in it would be severely punished. For demonstration effect, he sent home in shackles the hapless Zhu Jiyou, who had come to Nanjing to present with pride the fruits of his researches to the throne. The poor fellow was arrested and marched back to his home in Jiangxi province, where his house was ransacked and his papers burned. He was flogged a hundred strokes for good measure. The intimidation effect worked. Yongle's enshrinement of the Cheng-Zhu orthodoxy lasted through the Ming and into most of the Qing (1644–1912).

The Ming had, of course, been founded with the aid of freelance intellectuals, men like Liu Ji (1311–1375) and Song Lian (1310–1381), who were eclectic devotees of all learning, not narrow Cheng-Zhu apologists, and who felt themselves at liberty to digest and rethink the whole philosophical heritage of China and adapt it to the needs of the times. And in the same spirit, Fang Xiaoru (1357–1402) undertook yet again to think about China's past and future (and the immediate wreck Taizu had bequeathed to his successor, Jianwen) and engineer a nationwide decentralization based upon a classics-guided retooling of the whole Ming system. But Fang openly defied Yongle when the latter burst into Nanjing in 1402, and Yongle murdered him and everyone even remotely connected to him, as many as a thousand people in all. His works were, of course, banned. Such intellectual freedom as Ming China may have enjoyed under Taizu and Jianwen came to an abrupt and horrifying end. Zhu Jiyou should have taken note.

How could anything like intellectual activity survive in China after such repression? A truth-seeker by the name of Wu Yubi (1392–1469) had an answer: drop all further concern for the future of China and stay completely away from government and politics. Then, use the officially approved Neo-Confucian texts themselves to work up a personal program of psychic self-rectification with the achievement of sagehood (not official position) as the ultimate goal.

Wu's father was a high-ranking Nanjing official who in 1402 shifted his loyalty from Jianwen to Yongle. Like any other official's son, young Wu studied hard to try to pass the civil service examinations. Then something happened. He decided he would have no more of it. At the age of seventeen he left his father and went home to the little family farm in northern Jiangxi, there to spend the next half-century seeking sagehood while living the life of a peasant. Word of his example spread around. A steady stream of students came to his gate, many of them *shengyuan* who had had unhappy experiences with the exam system. Several of his students went on to achieve celebrity on their own as national guides to sagehood. One of them, Lou Liang (1422–1491), came briefly into the life of the young Wang Yangming (1472–1529), who visited him in Jiangxi in 1489. While Lou's recommendation for psychic reconstruction focused on the notion of "reverence" (*jing*), his message for Wang stressed Zhu Xi's dictum to "investigate things" (*gewu*), a precept Wang wrestled with but in the end rejected in his own search for sagehood. Another disciple of Wu's, Hu Juren (1434–1584), combined an intense focus on psychic self-cultivation with an interest in local institutions, especially private academies, in a sort of reprise of the pattern set by Zhu Xi (1130–1200) himself back in Southern Song times.

But no doubt Chen Xianzhang (1428–1500), from Guangdong province, was the most celebrated (and the least faithful) of Wu Yubi's circle of immediate disciples. Brilliant, but a repeated failure at the metropolitan exams, Chen visited Wu for several months in 1454, but he returned home to Guangdong dissatisfied. Wu was unable to show him the "entrance gate" to the truth and the Way. By now, however, the stifling atmosphere of repression that had shaped Wu Yubi's thought and behavior was beginning to dissipate. It was no longer so dangerous to venture beyond the orthodoxy.

Chen spent ten years in solitary meditation. Then one day he awoke to the joyous realization that psychic readjustment could not be learned from books or from the world round about, but could only come in a flash of revelation. That was arguably a Buddhist approach. But the effect on the self was decisive: by his own efforts, Chen had lifted himself to an inner mountaintop where neither wealth nor poverty nor honor nor degradation, nor heaven and earth or life and death could bother him any more in the slightest. His announced triumph impressed many, and he achieved a kind of national stardom, even among the officials, of whom several were fervent supporters. He also provoked the doubt and jealousy that stardom often entails.

Then Wang Yangming made a leap that was measurably beyond the benchmark Chen Xianzhang had just set. Unlike Chen, Wang had achieved the metropolitan (*jinshi*) degree, and went on to become an important and active and successful official. He was eager to multitask—that is, to weave philosophizing and teaching his many avid disciples into the very fabric of his official tasks, which by themselves were no light duty.

Wang won his *jinshi* in 1499 and served in various mid-level posts in Beijing until 1506 when he was flogged and blacklisted along with fifty-two other officials, and exiled to Guizhou for having taken part in a protest against the Zhengde emperor's eunuch entourage and its leader, Liu Jin. Restored to office after Liu Jin's execution, Wang spent the rest of his career in south China, as magistrate of Luling county, Jiangxi, and then as Grand Coordinator in far south China, 1516–1521, directing a large suppression campaign against outlaws, handling reconstruction and local reform, directing the campaign against the rebel Prince of Ning in 1519, all the while welcoming all sorts of students and admirers who were eager to meet him, hear his message, and watch him at work. Wang spent the years 1521–1527 at home, thinking, lecturing, and counseling many hundreds of students. He was recalled in 1527 to serve again as Grand Coordinator, this time to suppress a tribal rebellion in Guizhou. He died, of what may have been tuberculosis, a year and a half later.

Wang's impact on young strivers was electrifying. They could visit him or learn about him by word of mouth or they could read his *Chuanxi lu*, consisting of personal letters and recorded conversations, and published in installments during his lifetime. Key to all of it were Wang's formulae, argued from the inherited Confucian doctrines, for engaging the psychically readjusted mind with the world round about in such a way that positive results followed. Knowledge, Wang argued, didn't precede action; it *was* action. Mind did not just reflect the universe; it *was* the universe. The mind must engage the world and society in such a way that when one "extended one's good conscience" (*zhi liangzhi*)—that is, radiated one's inner sense of moral and psychic integrity outward, then others sensed that and could be swept away by it. In practice, this was not an easy formula, and only certain kinds of extroverted personalities could effectively make it work. Wang insisted, unconvincingly, that none of his teachings contradicted Zhu Xi.[1]

Sixteenth-century China, especially the Jiajing era (1522–1567), featured, as one side effect of a rising prosperity, a remarkable burst of private academy building. Wang Yangming's friendly philosophical rival Zhan Ruoshui (1466–1560) sponsored the construction of some thirty-six of them, in memory of his teacher, Chen Xianzhang, mainly in his native Guangdong province and in the southern metropolitan region. Wang Yangming (and after his death, his disciples) likewise propagated his teachings in discussion-group meetings held in local academies newly founded for the purpose, many of them in Jiangxi province, where Wang spent much of his career. Local philanthropists and enthusiasts were heavily involved in funding construction. In Beijing, the Jiajing emperor and many of his top officials greeted this activity with suspicion and hostility, but they did little about it (except, perhaps, to try to raise the competitive attractiveness of the local government schools by restocking and expanding their book collections).

Indeed, a new and more liberal dispensation, inadvertently inspired by Jiajing's views on family ritual, and encouraged further by Wang and Zhan and their many followers, swept through sixteenth-century China—erasing hierarchies, blurring social class distinctions, loosening rules, and engendering new social networks.

By way of illustration, probably the most influential of Wang Yangming's many adherents was the irrepressibly sincere Wang Gen (1483–1541), who grew up poor and only partly educated in Taizhou (on the north side of the Yangzi River, near the coast). He did well as a young salt merchant, however. In 1509, at the age of twenty-six, he visited the shrine of Confucius in Qufu, Shandong province, and there had a vision of himself as a Confucian sage. Ten years later, he considered himself ready to start a career as an evangelist, his message being that the Confucian Way was available to everyone—old, young, wise, naïve, of high rank or lowly station, it didn't matter. In 1520 he traveled to Jiangxi to meet Wang Yangming, already famous for his precept to "extend the good conscience." Normally, someone of Wang Yangming's power and status would have brushed off a lowly figure like Wang Gen, but the latter's unusually extroverted sincerity won Wang Yangming over. He made Wang Gen stop some of his eccentricities, but admitted him into his inner circle. After Wang Yangming's death in 1529, Wang Gen went on to attract many friends and listeners—from officials to woodcutters and servants and children—and found a school of his own, the so-called Taizhou school named after his own area. There even a certain boy of ten, the son of a local official, was deeply impressed by Wang's promise of sagehood to anyone who developed an appropriate love of self and others.

Luo Rufang (1515–1588) was every bit as ardent a seeker of sagehood as Wang Gen, but he achieved the *jinshi* degree and served capably as a local and regional official until he ran afoul of Chief Grand Secretary Zhang Juzheng in 1579. Luo is much better known for his other career—as an inspiring, indeed charismatic lecturer who appeared regularly before large mixed audiences of literati, rich people, and untutored commoners, always delivering an uplifting and resolutely optimistic message of ethical self-realization. Well-known sixteenth-century Confucian teachers and enlighteners were interconnected, either having studied under each other or at least having hearsay knowledge of each other's sayings and doings. Thus Luo Rufang knew about Wang Gen through a disciple of one of Wang Gen's disciples (Xu Yue, *jinshi* of 1532). That person was a strange, mesmerizing character named Yan Jun, with the sobriquet "Mountain Farmer," an uneducated fellow but in his prime a compelling moral instructor who counseled the young Luo, who had made himself ill seeking sagehood. Yan said it was not enough to stop one's desires; one had to go further and "embody benevolence." Luo took Yan Jun as his master, bailed him out of prison in 1568, and put him up in his own home as a kind of live-in holy man, acquiescing to the end in Yan's increasingly bizarre and abusive behavior, a posture of humility that won for Luo wide admiration.

In his better days, Yan Jun was an apostle of goodness-driven spontaneity. If human beings were by definition morally good, then they should have no self-doubts, no self-restraint, but freely do whatever prompted them. Yan himself went to extreme lengths to help others in trouble. A Jiangxi co-provincial, He Xinyin (1517–1579), met Yan Jun soon after winning his provincial *juren* degree (first place winner in Jiangxi in 1546). He fell under Yan's spell and dropped any idea of proceeding further with an official career. Building on the legacy of ideas developed by Wang Yangming, Wang Gen, and Yan Jun, he pioneered and led an extraordinary private campaign of his own to transcend self, family, and state and reorder Ming society as a collectivity of interlinked friends gathered in schools and academies and engaging in free "discussion and study" (*jiangxue*). For eighteen years, He Xinyin traveled all over China, from Beijing (which he fled in 1561, fearing arrest for his part in a plot to discredit the Chief Grand Secretary, Yan Song) to cities and other locales south of the Yangzi, from Fujian on the coast to Sichuan in the deep interior and many stops in between. In 1579 he was arrested, not for the first time. What was he up to, organizing a rebellion? Officials eager to curry favor with Chief Grand Secretary Zhang Juzheng, who was outspokenly hostile to *jiangxue*, flogged him to death. In the same year, Zhang ordered academies nationwide closed.

In order to thrive, the *jiangxue* ("discussion and study") movement clearly needed to find shielding by or from high officialdom in Beijing. Xu Jie (1503–1583), grand secretary from 1552 to 1562, then chief grand secretary from 1562 to 1568, had provided that protection, as he himself was a confessed convert to Wang Yangming's teachings. It was, he said, Ouyang De (1496–1554, minister of rites from 1552 and a former personal disciple of Wang Yangming's) who had made a convert of him. Interestingly, both he and Ouyang De, as followers of Wang, could and did find ways to play the often unpleasant and underhanded bureaucratic power game while at the same time serving credibly as supporters of and participants in *jiangxue*. As grand secretary, Xu Jie arranged giant *jiangxue* gatherings in 1553 and 1554 at the Lingji Temple, a spacious Daoist structure in the northwest part of Beijing, and placed in charge of the meetings Ouyang De and Nie Bao (1487–1563, a former mentor of his and minister of war, 1553–1555). These meetings were timed to take advantage of the presence in Beijing of several thousand *jinshi* examination candidates. Xu Jie himself was persuaded to lead another such gathering in 1558, but it wasn't as successful. In 1565, Luo Rufang gave a rousing speech at the temple, apparently at Xu Jie's behest. Such were the high-water marks of the coalescence of *jiangxue* with political power.[2]

But the great wave of Wang Yangming–inspired *jiangxue* crested and flattened as much due to the exhaustion of its own message of moral spontaneity, as to the forcible suppression imposed by Zhang Juzheng in 1579. A younger generation of people abandoned *jiangxue* along with the uncritical belief in the positive effects of radiating inner goodness. A widespread hunger for spiritual fulfillment persisted, however, and there were other ways to satisfy it.

While Confucian evangelism was a spent force after a half-century in vogue, other contemporaneous moral and religious movements developed greater organizational strength and a more lasting hold on people's loyalties. For instance, a popularized form of Buddhism arose and spread among the boatmen along the Grand Canal. It developed a network of hostels and an appealing doctrine that urged everyone to drop all social differences and seek the Buddha's Pure Land in oneself through meditation. Called the "Luo Teaching" after Luo Qing, its early sixteenth-century founder, it spread from the Grand Canal all along the coast, and although government was suspicious of it, the religion won converts among the rich and literate as well as among the poor. Then there was Lin Zhaoen (1517–1598), son of a scholar-official family of Fujian, whose career defied all the usual categories. When he was a child, his father introduced him to Wang Yangming. After his third failed attempt to pass the provincial exams, he gave up, and following a vision that came to him in a dream, turned himself into the chief theologian and head organizer of an amalgamated Confucian-Buddhist-Daoist church of his own. Just as Wang Gen had once done, Lin too went so far as to design and wear special vestments. He became an honored prophet both at home (where he and his congregation extended charity and helped out with anti-pirate defense) as well as on the road, as he traveled through Jiangxi, Zhejiang, and Nanjing drawing large crowds and winning admirers and converts wherever he went. His admirers included such luminaries as Qi Jiguang (the military expert) and He Xinyin (the Confucian organizer of academies). Lin's organized church lasted into modern times, but for some reason it became confined to Fujian and to Fujianese émigré communities in Southeast Asia. Thus an ability to persist organizationally over time did not necessarily give a church or a sect more than a local or regional presence in the large realm that was China. The Catholic Church in China, introduced to Ming China in the late sixteenth century, was also a durable phenomenon, but it suffered this sort of limitation as well.[3]

A revived elitist Buddhism spread further, if not deeper. It may be significant that just as the *jiangxue* movement faded in the 1580s, the emotional and spiritual intensity that had once been invested in it was resumed by a new generation, born in the 1530s and 1540s, who found in Buddhism a compelling vehicle for their spiritual needs. Jiajing's patronage of Daoism was abruptly scrapped at his death in 1567. When his successor, the Longqing emperor, died in 1572, his consort, the formidable Empress Li (1546–1614), mother of the child emperor Wanli, became a fervent patron and sponsor of Buddhism. (She made Wanli declare Zhu Changluo heir apparent, and send Zhu Changxun out to a princedom in Henan, and so she was in the good graces of the "good species" or Donglin faction in the outer court.)

Empress Li spent freely from the funds collected by Wanli's extortion-ate eunuch tax collectors. She sponsored the extraordinary priest and construction magnate Fudeng (1540–1613), a northerner of very humble origin, who built or restored temples, pagodas, bridges, halls, rest houses, and free clinics all over north China, Sichuan, and the southern metropolitan province. In 1581–1582, he and his friend Deqing (1546–1623) took up quarters at the Wutai shan Buddhist center in Shanxi, copied out the *Avatamsaka sūtra* in their own blood, and then organized a mass gathering of religious and laypeople that lasted for four months. At the request of Empress Li, they prayed that Wanli would produce an heir (which he did: Zhu Changluo was born in August 1582). Deqing, a lifelong monk from an obscure central China family, was a spellbinding lecturer who, in the 1570s, had been drawing daily audiences of thousands to his presentations at one of the Wutai shan monasteries. Partisans of Wanli's beloved concubine, Lady Zheng, and her son, Zhu Changxun, managed in 1586 to get Deqing arrested and exiled to military service in Guangdong. But local authorities let Deqing travel about the south, and in 1605, he was released, to great acclaim. Highly literate, Deqing was friendly with several of the leading lights in the Confucian Donglin faction.

The monk Zhenke (1544–1604) fared less well. He was also a leading figure in the late Ming Buddhist revival. He hailed from Wujiang, a county south of Suzhou in the southern metropolitan region. He and Deqing met in 1586 and became friends. Learned and extremely devout, Zhenke's career ended when he went to Beijing in 1601 to make a plea for Deqing's release from exile. But he went too far when he also protested Wanli's eunuch mining intendants. He knew personally of the tragic harm they caused. For that he was imprisoned. But he had friends in bureaucracy—people such as Lu Guangzu whom we met in the previous chapter—and he was released. Then he was imprisoned again in connection with Wanli's angry retaliation against officials who, he believed, were indirectly charging him with unfilial behavior toward his mother, Empress Li. Zhenke died from the effects of the flogging he got in the notorious Decree Prison, the facility run by the Embroidered-Uniform Guard.

Zhuhong (1544–1604), from Hangzhou in Zhejiang province, married but childless, and a repeated exam failure, gave it all up in 1566 and entered the Buddhist priesthood. For five years he traveled extensively, visiting Buddhist centers, after which he returned home where he stayed for the rest of his life, after 1577, in a temple, the Yunqi si, that he and the local literati rebuilt and restored. Zhuhong's interests were different from those of Fudeng, Deqing, and Zhenke. He imposed an iron discipline on the monks housed in the Yunqi si, necessary because monks were commonly despised in late Ming for their idleness and corruption, and Zhuhong's was a revival movement. Zhuhong was not interested in reforming and rebuilding the entire Buddhist church, however. Rather, his aim was to attract laypeople, local elites especially, to Buddhism, by way of creating charities, conducting public rituals to ward off epidemics and droughts, and organizing animal-releasing ceremonies. In this he was successful, and his example inspired imitators in other parts of south China. Indeed, Timothy Brook has argued that by funding, patronizing, and taking part in Buddhist ceremonies and charities, late Ming local literati were affirming their status as elites while at the same time avoiding entangling themselves with local government.[4]

Buddhists competed with the priests of the new religion of Catholic Christianity for converts; in 1608, Zhuhong wrote an angry response to an anti-Buddhist publication of Matteo Ricci's.

Buddhism's effect on people's minds could take various forms. The literati might imbibe it in a cool form, as philosophy, or in a hot form, as religion. In this connection, I should like to cite an intriguingly detailed example, that of Wang Erkang (1567–1604) of Luling county in Jiangxi. As a child he was silent, given to sitting cross-legged, Buddhist-style, pretending to chant from scripture. People thought him retarded. At twelve, he was living in Peizhou in Sichuan province, where his father was a subprefectural magistrate, when he spotted a Buddhist text, the *Yuanjue jing*, on a table. He leafed through it. His father asked him if he understood it. "I do," he replied, even though he had not yet learned to read and usually just looked at books for their pictures. So his father picked out a passage and asked the child to explain it. At first, he could not answer; but after a while, he felt something like a knife or axe splitting open his chest, whereat he became bright and intelligent and began speaking in a way that was profound and abstruse, which amazed his father. From then on, his powers of understanding text were so sharp that for him it was like walking down a street and being able to see clearly into the furthest interiors of all the houses.

Wang Erkang did not, however, become a monk. He passed his provincial exams in 1591, and his *jinshi* in 1594, and for the rest of his disease-shortened life he served as an imperial messenger, a low-ranking post that did enable him to travel and visit famous monasteries.

Among the stories told about Wang was this one: One night while he was off by himself in a pavilion chanting the *Avatamsaka sūtra*, his wife dreamt that the sun like a great wheel hung right over the pavilion where her husband was, so bright she couldn't look directly at it. She then awoke, and told Wang of her dream. Wang told her that this was a great directive from the dharma of the Buddha. His wife, overjoyed, thereupon became a vegetarian and lived in purity until she died, in 1601, her life, sadly, also a short one. This is just one of countless ways in which the Buddhist revival could impact the lives of late Ming laypeople, degree-holding officials and their wives among them.[5]

From about the mid-sixteenth century, the literate local elites and many of the officials of Ming China began turning away from well-defined schools of thought (such as those derived from Zhu Xi or Wang Yangming), and from government-directed solutions to social and other kinds of problems as well. The grand utopian state-centered vision of early Ming was all but dead. Even the more modest state-centered programs of later times, such as the nationwide famine insurance granary program launched in 1440, with the state offering official titles and service exemptions to big local grain donors, disappeared as well. The literati began filling the gap by devoting funds and efforts to piecemeal local improvement projects. There is a likelihood that the "Single Whip" tax reforms, the cumulative result of a large number of local changes made during the sixteenth century, shared ideological and organizational space plus a certain congruity with the shift toward individualism and localism that characterized literati preoccupations more generally.

While the Buddhist revival was in progress, some leading members of the intelligentsia adopted a strategy of bringing about sociomoral improvement not in the old way, through collective institutions such as schools and academies and *jiangxue*, or through religion, but by retailing self-improvement programs to people individually. An outstanding proponent of this approach was Yuan Huang (1533–1606), an official with expertise also in frontier defense, sea transport, county administration, and various other matters. (Like the monk Zhenke, he came from Wujiang county south of Suzhou.) Yuan Huang prepared a number of publications aimed at the growing population of struggling *shengyuan*, including study aids for the examinations. But he also championed an efficacious approach to self-improvement by way of keeping a daily diary of one's good and bad deeds. The idea was to develop one's merits and enhance one's chances for success in life and career. (The Buddhist monk Zhuhong advocated the very same thing.) Indeed, "goodness books" (*shan shu*) sold very well on the popular market. Beyond this, there further developed a new genre of scathingly critical autobiography, as writers responded to the rediscovery of evil in the world and in themselves by dropping the old habit of reticence in such matters and turning to anguished introspection, confession, and self-reproach. This was a full turn away from the idea of "extending the good conscience" that Wang Yangming and his school had propagated through much of the earlier part of the sixteenth century.[6]

The general trend toward individualism and localism had yet other manifestations. Individualistic, because he subscribed to no school and recognized no master, Lü Kun (1536–1618) was a northerner from Ningling county east of Kaifeng in Henan province. Lü had a long career in local and provincial government in north China, and in the Ministries of Personnel and Justice and in the Censorate in Beijing. His famous memorial of 1597, which directly excoriated the policies and behavior of the Wanli emperor, led to his dismissal, and he spent the rest of his life at home. (Wanli was less inclined than his grandfather Jiajing to imprison and flog his detractors.) Lü Kun gained fame through his writings. He was interested in the question of how government through its officials should readdress its deteriorating relationship with society at large. His brief was that officials needed to put aside their emphasis on abstract moral ideals and instead study in all seriousness ground-level facts about the people, their wants and needs, and respond to those with understanding and compassion. It was wrongheaded, he thought, to condemn people for their greed and self-interest; officials, like kindly doctors, should combine their expertise with all due regard for their patients and their ailments. All this was state-centered and authoritarian, but it was a sign of a growing interest among the intelligentsia in practical administration—an interest that, among other things, prompted the publication of the *Huang Ming jingshi wenbian* in 1638.

As a perception spread among the literati that Ming governance at the local level was eroding and unraveling, the more affluent among them began engaging in local fact-centered works at their own initiative, in large measure bypassing local government rather than trying to change it. An example of this sort of endeavor is Lü Kun's co-provincial and friend Yang Dongming, from Yucheng, about twenty-five miles east of Ningling. Like Lü, Yang was an ex-official and wealthy landowner. Yang made energetic contributions to local education, poor relief, disaster relief, and local transportation infrastructure. Also, he organized larger assemblies (*hui*) of all the Yucheng elites who shared his interests in charitable works and local education.

It might be argued that as long as well-off literati deflected likely sources of hostility by caring and charitable giving, late Ming society was willing to turn a blind eye to any unorthodox and novel ways of thought they might harbor. This supposition might help explain the case of Li Zhi (1527–1602), late Ming China's most notorious and much discussed iconoclast, then and now. Li was a brilliant writer and conversationalist—in short, an intellectual. Because he held only the provincial degree, not the *jinshi*, he was assigned a series of low and middling posts, all of them disagreeable to him, and so he quit government in 1581 and devoted the rest of his life to literary work and to publishing. He never went home to Fujian province to live the life of a local benefactor. Just the opposite: he seems to have subsisted on the generosity of far-away friends.

First he stayed with the Geng brothers in Huang'an county in northern Huguang (nowadays Hubei province). In 1585 he and Geng Dingxiang (1524–1596) had a serious falling-out, so he sent his unloved wife back to Fujian, shaved his head Buddhist-style to show he had cut all family ties (of his eight children, only one daughter survived), and moved to neighboring Macheng county where he took up residence in a large Buddhist resort and inn. This inn, the Zhifo yuan, became a major gathering-place for some of the leading literary and philosophical lights of the time, the so-called Dragon Lake group. Nationally known scholar-officials Zhou Sirui and Zhou Sijing and Ma Guozhen (1542–1605), natives of Macheng, sponsored and funded all this. It is a characteristic of late Ming China that a movement such as this could take place in Macheng, so far from Beijing or Nanjing or Suzhou or any of the great cities of the realm.

Li Zhi, despite a thin connection to the Wang Yangming and Taizhou schools and his staunch championing of the imprisoned He Xinyin, was no practitioner of "extending the good conscience." Quite the opposite, he was arrogant, intensely friendly with those few whom he considered his intellectual equals, and coldly dismissive of everyone else. He revered the original Confucius of the *Analects*, but reviled nearly everything said or done in Confucius's name in the two thousand years since his death, including Zhu Xi and the whole Neo-Confucian program. He offended everyone protective of the status quo. He was accused of womanizing. This sort of behavior ignited angry passions.

Geng Dingxiang, once a friend, became an implacable enemy. He threatened physical violence. Old as he was, Li at first vowed to brave it out. But in 1601, the Macheng magistrate, at the behest of influential locals, organized a mob to destroy the Zhifo yuan. Li fled. He escaped north to Henan province where a friend, Ma Jinglun, who was a censor, offered him protection and brought him with him to his post at Tongzhou, near Beijing. There in 1602, another censor impeached him as a likely source of social and moral disorder. He was arrested. In prison Li committed suicide by slitting his throat.[7]

A prolific author of historical and other works, Li in his personal life strove for personal liberation from the restraints of family, of bureaucratic life, from the demands of charity, from anything traditional and rule-bound. But another, very different current was working its way among the literati of late Ming China.

In 1604, two years after Li Zhi's suicide, Gu Xiancheng (1550–1612) and Gao Panlong (1562–1626) restored a Song-era academy, the Donglin, in Wuxi, a county southeast of Nanjing, as a venue for *jiangxue*. The government a quarter-century before had closed down the practice of "discussing and learning." However, its provocative revival was not an attempt to revive the precepts of Wang Yangming. The Donglin restorers' aim was to reconcile the divergent paths Wang and orthodox Cheng-Zhu Neo-Confucianism had taken, but on the whole favoring Zhu Xi. Gao Panlong also provided charity for the county's poor and needy. Donglin thought offered little that was new; instead, it resuscitated older beliefs in the reality of evil, the need for discipline

and restraint on one's freewheeling inclinations, and in the necessary dissocia-
tion or non-identity of mind with the world round about.

Why did this shopworn set of ideas catch on among the students and
junior officials of the late Ming as though it were a wind-driven blaze
through dry grass? It did catch on. The Donglin was soon joined by several
other academies that friends and colleagues of Gu and Gao were inspired to
build—in Shaanxi, in Jiangxi, and in the southern metropolitan region, and
eventually even in Beijing itself. These academies were not so much schools
as gathering places for officials, local literati, students, and visiting lecturers
for the purpose of "discussing study." What energized the Donglin movement
were not so much ideas in the abstract, as the immediate relevance of those
ideas to politics. "Discussion" included the analysis of the current political
malaise, the targeting of evil officials, and the mobilization of men and opinion in an all-out effort to make things right again in China.

This was far from Wang Yangming's disbelief in confrontation, and his
insistence on a slower and gentler approach to effecting change, by radiating one's inner goodness. The Donglin would effect change by more violent
means. Donglin activists shared a robust and self-righteous moral absolutism.
They divided officialdom into two opposed camps (menhu): "gentlemen"
(junzi) and "small men" (xiao ren). Gentlemen were those who stood up for
the public good. Small men cravenly chased profit and personal advantage.
The Donglin line was that ever since Zhang Juzheng's time, a quarter-
century before, small men had been running China, which was why it was
now in such a sorry condition. A big purge of the current regime of small
men in central positions and their replacement by gentlemen would, with
the emperor's blessing, save China from its almost certain disintegration
and collapse. Carrying out this purge demanded that the gentlemen act in
concert, even as a partisan group (dang), and use their large arsenal of verbal
pyrotechnics to assail the incumbent small men and, absolutely essential,
convince the emperor of their own unselfish concern for the dynasty's fate.

The gentlemen girded themselves as if for war. One of their leaders, Zou
Yuanbiao (1551–1624), urged the younger men to expect poverty and defa-
mation; to think of themselves as pines enduring the winter blasts, not plum
trees that bloom for a moment; and not to shrink from tasks that looked
impossible. The "heart and guts" (xin chang) that the ancient sages had once
exhibited would see them through to victory.

The great moment for the Donglin faction arrived with the enthronement of the ill-fated Taichang emperor in the summer of 1620. Under his
successor, the boy Tianqi emperor, they lost momentum, and in 1625–1626
suffered literally bloody defeat as their foes, the "small men," stung by the

excoriation and humiliation the Donglin had heaped on them, got help from palace eunuch Wei Zhongxian. Tianqi authorized the arrest, imprisonment, and daily flogging of twelve leading members of the Donglin party at the hands of the Embroidered-Uniform Guard. The Guard finally murdered all twelve, probably on secret orders. A thirteenth leader, Donglin co-founder Gao Panlong, expecting arrest, committed suicide at home. Hundreds of other officials, suspected of Donglin ties, were dismissed from government. All the offending academies were closed down and their assets confiscated. The victors at once published an official account of the whole affair, in the mistaken belief that they could reclaim the moral high ground and convince the people of China that they had done the right thing in rescuing the dynasty from so many villainous blackguards. (The death of Tianqi in 1628 and the enthronement of Chongzhen partly reversed this settlement, as noted in chapter 2.)[8]

As a phoenix rising from the ashes, the Fushe ("Restoration Society"), organized by literati across much of China, took the place of the Donglin in national affairs shortly after Chongzhen's enthronement. It was in some ways a continuation of the Donglin, but under new leaders, as the Donglin leaders were dead. The main leader of this new movement was the young and extraordinarily energetic Zhang Pu (1602–1641), from Taicang county in the southern metropolitan province. The Fushe was more a political machine than a philosophical movement. It stood for ethical probity and administrative competence, but its whole purpose was to act as a kind of labor union and lobby higher officials on behalf of the more promising of the degree-seeking mass of local licentiates (*shengyuan*), whom they had vetted. The Fushe provided these promising candidates with patronage and help in writing effective examination essays. All over China, but mainly in the richer southeastern parts, local students had for a long time formed small groups to help each other in their studies and exam preparations. The Fushe developed into an umbrella organization embracing some hundreds of such local "literary societies" (*wen she*) with two and eventually three thousand members. General convocations of all the groups were held in 1629, in 1630 in Nanjing, and in 1632 near Suzhou. Zhang Pu made his own home in Taicang command headquarters. There, he and his large staff raised funds, conducted membership drives, and published model examination essays for members to use as study material. Zhang Pu, precocious and obviously charismatic, had a definite mission in mind. He made important contacts when he visited Beijing in 1628, and again in 1631, when he won his *jinshi* degree. But he declined to take an official position. He chose to go back home and use those contacts to enhance his work as a Fushe organizer. He and others lobbied to get officials who sympathized with them appointed as readers and graders in the triennial provincial and metropolitan exams. This worked. Fushe members enjoyed impressive rates of success. Unfortunately but understandably, their success provoked angry controversy and yet another sad chapter in the long saga of late Ming partisan conflict.

The end of the Ming was not far off, and we will not pursue the story beyond this point. But it might be noted that the Ming experience with literati self-organization—the *jiangxue* movement in the private academies of the sixteenth century and the Donglin and Fushe circles of the seventeenth— was a historical dead end. The Qing prohibited all such activities as threats to security and order. Literati interests and energies had to be channeled in other directions altogether.[9]

～

But there were other ways to gather literati. The dangers and terrors of political mobilization might be avoided. Confucian ideology, centered on the Cheng-Zhu orthodoxy or the Wang Yangming alternative, was not to everyone's taste. Nor were the stormy seas of administration. Buddhism didn't suit everyone. There was still a way for the literati legally to create a friendly and welcoming atmosphere for individuals and satisfy their need for self-fulfillment, however: to form loose gatherings of like-minded people around this or that style of literary expression.

In the very early Ming, the line between the leading men of ideas and those with literary ability and interests was not so sharply drawn as it later became. Song Lian (1310–1381) was an excellent prose stylist, extremely erudite, and philosophically eclectic. Liu Ji (1311–1375) was an all-round genius, a major thinker who influenced the whole nature and structure of the early Ming state, a compelling storyteller, and a poet of great talent. Liu Ji was beyond all imitation. Song Lian professed to transmit a sacred legacy— *siwen*, "this culture of ours"—to his chief disciple Fang Xiaoru (1357–1402), whose great ambition was to reconstruct Ming China institutionally in the light of his understanding of the Confucian classics. Fang commanded great powers of literary expression as well. But the Yongle emperor had him and thousands of others murdered shortly after his entry in Nanjing in 1402, and that ended all further pretense that the Confucian Way (*dao*) and literary expression (*wen*) could ever again be fruitfully conjoined in some protean effort to remake the world.

Another outstanding literary talent of the time was Gao Qi (1336– 1374), central figure in a literary and artistic circle based in Suzhou that came into prominence during the time Ming Taizu's rival, the warlord Zhang Shicheng, occupied that city. Noted for his poetry based partly on Tang models, Gao Qi had a taste for swashbuckling—it was called *youxia* or "knight-errantry"—that seemed to suit the world-remaking proclivities of the Ming founder. But not so. Recruited into Ming service as an editor, despite his reluctance to serve, Taizu executed him in 1374 on suspicion of a hidden loyalty toward Zhang Shicheng. Still, Gao Qi's fame has endured to the present day. But his death effectively suppressed further tendencies toward heroic expressions in poetry.

The earliest influential literary mode to affect Ming China after the Yongle takeover was the much more modest formulation of the so-called "Grand Secretariat style" (*taige ti*), championed by grand secretaries Yang Shiqi (1365–1444) and Li Dongyang (1447–1516). Li was the last grand secretary to dominate the literary scene. The style was not heroic, but reticent, straightforward, and uncontrived, tending to blandness. But it could be powerfully effective. To see that, one needs to consider an overlooked early exemplar of that style, one Liu Song (1321–1381), who came from the same county in Jiangxi province as Yang Shiqi. Liu's story is compelling.

Liu Song, together with his father and two brothers, owned a small farm in the countryside in central Jiangxi, but they were mainly tutors by trade, traveling up and down the Gan River valley, staying for a few months at a time in the homes of rich families with school-age children. Liu Song was attracted very early to poetry. At the age of eighteen, while he was working as a primary school teacher, someone showed him examples of the poems of the great Jiangxi writers of the time, Yu Ji (1272–1348) and Fan Chun. After reading them, Liu came to the sudden realization that poems must be simple and direct, that each one should convey some thought or idea, that they should arise from personal experience and articulate themselves in concrete representations, avoiding all literary artifice and allusion.

Liu stayed true to that approach. The editors of the *Siku quanshu* of Qing times were happy to copy over two thousand poems of his into that great imperial library. Indeed, reading them now, they come across as vivid descriptive comments, almost photographic. There was a lot for Liu to describe and comment on: the incessant fighting and marauding that ravaged the Gan River valley in the 1350s and '60s; the Jiangxi landscape, wild and domestic; hunting dogs in action; celebratory parades; public prayers for rain; military training exercises; the desolate and dust-blown landscape of north China; dawn court assemblies in Nanjing conducted in person by Taizu—the list is endless. Yet Liu's work is emotionally reserved. There is nothing heroic in it. He was witness to horrible things: the deaths of his two little sons from diarrhea and bloat while the family fled for safety from ravaging warlord troops;

the premature death of his wife; the destruction of his small farm; escape routes strewn with corpses. He described all this in unforgettable detail. Yet he deliberately avoided morbidity or pessimism, as he pointed out by way of praise for a younger man's poetic work as being "far from the tone of those who sit in remote seclusion, wailing sadly and thinking bitter thoughts, vainly laboring to find just the right word or line."

Liu Song cared deeply about his literary reputation, and did all he could to ensure that his written work was preserved for posterity. But about his career in the Ming—as Director of the Bureau of Operations in the Ministry of War; Surveillance Vice Commissioner for Beiping (site of the future capital of Beijing); Vice Minister of Rites; Acting Minister of Personnel; and finally, as a seriously ill man, Director of Studies in the Imperial University—he was reticent. He described vividly the daily pressures and anxieties and settings of his Ming service, but about his accomplishments in his tasks he said nothing. Yet from other sources we know that Taizu, not a man easy to please, appreciated his work as an official and held him in high regard personally for his conscientiousness and assiduity.[10]

As for the Grand Secretarial style, its death was hastened on by politics. The coda for it was Grand Secretary Li Dongyang's widely condemned decision to stand aside in the great court demonstration of 1506 staged against the Zhengde emperor's eunuch entourage. (Blame for the failure of that demonstration, and the emergence of the eunuch dictator Liu Jin, was imputed to the cowardice if not collusion of the Grand Secretary.)

A new literary movement emerged from the rubble. A prime mover in that same court demonstration, Li Mengyang (1473–1529), a former protégé of the Grand Secretary, was the leading light in a circle that came to be known later as the "Seven Early Masters." The practitioners of the *taige ti* had looked to Song and Yuan models for their work. The new group rejected all those and looked instead to the Western Han for prose and the high Tang for poetry. "All the literati," notes the Ming dynastic history, "who were devoted to writing and discussing the arts followed them, and Ming prose and poetry underwent a profound change."

This change took place at about the same time that Wang Yangming and his admirers were making their mark. However, Li Mengyang and his circle were mainly northerners, while Wang and his were predominantly from the south. The only southerner among the Seven Early Masters was Xu Zhenqing (1479–1511) of Taicang, who was simultaneously one of an incandescent southern coterie, the "Four Talents of Wu," that included Tang Yin (1470–1524), a Suzhou man, disqualified for cheating on the civil service exams, who then turned to carousing, poetry, womanizing, and art; Wen Zhenming (1470–1559), also of Suzhou, the greatest artist of his time, and by recommendation (not exams) given a low post in the Hanlin Academy during 1523–1525, his only experience with officialdom; and Zhu Yunming (1461–1527), a provincial degree-holder who did fine work for a few years as a local magistrate, but who was better known for his calligraphy and for his iconoclastic attacks on the Cheng-Zhu orthodoxy and on accepted interpretations of China's history. In this, he prefigured Li Zhi. Just as Wang Yangming's movement attracted bizarre figures from the social and intellectual fringe (Wang Gen and Yan Jun, for example), so here too a literary circle formed by mid-level officials in Beijing shaded off to draw in highly talented but marginal and offbeat characters in Suzhou.[11]

The next literary generation, known loosely as the "Eight Talents," rejected the Western Han and high Tang standards approved by the Early Seven Masters, in favor of early Tang models for poetry and Northern Song ones for prose. One of the leaders in this development was the brilliant and irrepressible Tang Shunzhi (1507–1560), a polymath and activist with interests in everything under the sun. From Wujin in the southern metropolitan region, he dallied for a time in the Wang Yangming school, followed Li Dongyang and the Early Seven Masters, then found all that too constraining, as his interests moved on to include astronomy, mathematics, weapons, and military strategy. Tang won the *jinshi* degree in 1529, and was assigned to the Hanlin Academy, but he was too self-willed, eccentric, and ascetic to be content patiently to climb the bureaucratic ladder. Poor health was his excuse to spend most of his time back in the south, writing and publishing. In 1558, on a whim, he volunteered to join the staff of Hu Zongxian (1511–1565), then based in Hangzhou as Regional Inspector and playing a major operational role in the ongoing battle against the Wokou (pirates). Hu was also a bon vivant, commercial entrepreneur, and one of the earliest literati-officials to recognize and publish short stories written in a popular style—just the sort of man to attract Tang Shunzhi. Tang didn't just sit idly in headquarters, however; he insisted on a hands-on role in the fighting. Unfortunately for his reputation, he was inept as a fighter.

That leads us to Xu Wei (1521–1593), not a member of any particular literary circle, but a friend of Tang Shunzhi's. An eight-time failure at the exams, he became a professional writer and dramatist in his native Shaoxing, Zhejiang province. Hu Zongxian added him to his anti-pirate staff as an advisor, and there he and Tang became acquainted. In 1565, Hu Zongxian was arrested and imprisoned. Xu Wei went berserk with fear. He castrated himself. He beat his wife to death. He then spent seven years in prison. Zhang Yuanbian (1538–1588), a local compatriot and Hanlin official, helped win his release. Xu Wei, meanwhile, seems to have recovered from his bout of mental illness. He returned to writing, painting, calligraphy, and giving military advice, this time at Xuanfu, on the northern frontier. (And from his story one sees the mutual entanglement of all the themes raised in this book—land and ocean frontiers, governance, literati . . .)

Among the Eight Talents, the only northerner was Li Kaixian (1502–1568), of Zhangqiu in Shandong province. Dismissed from office in 1541, he returned home to create a large estate featuring a library, a school, and publishing facilities for the drama and other works he composed. He hated the blind imitation of models from the past. He valued individuality and originality. Strange, then, that he should have been as close as he was to two seniors who were northern members of the Early Seven Masters—Kang Hai (1475–1541), a dramatist, lute-player, patron of songstresses, and bitter critic of officialdom; and Wang Jiusi (1458–1551), also a fine dramatist, with whom Li cooperated in producing work in the Southern Song poem style, *sanqu*, that was new for northern readers. The venom expressed by Kang and Wang against Li Dongyang and the other adherents of the disgraced *taige ti* (Grand Secretariat style) was real, but the boundaries of the Early Seven Masters group were clearly porous.

The Eight Talents directly inspired other southern luminaries, such as Gui Youguang (1507–1571) of Kunshan east of Suzhou, and Mao Kun (1512–1601) of Guian in Zhejiang. The trajectory of Mao's stormy career resembled that of Tang Shunzhi. Gui Youguang's self-pitying writings were widely read by local licentiates because they expressed so well their own frustrations and difficulties with the examination system.[12]

A by-now anticipated reaction to the literary climate developed by the Eight Talents gradually coalesced around a new group that in time came to be known as the Seven Later Masters. Among them, the most prominent figure by far was Wang Shizhen (1526–1590), of Taicang in the southern metropolitan province. This group began taking form in 1547, when Wang won his *jinshi* degree, ingratiated himself with several poetry-minded senior officials, and also joined together with year-mates and other younger men with literary talents and interests. When the senior leader, Li Panlong, died in 1570, Wang stepped forward to serve as China's supreme literary arbiter and critic until his own death in 1590.

Just what did this mean? Wang turned out a gigantic pile of writing—poems, occasional pieces, works on Ming history, all of it good, but none of it particularly memorable. Intermittently he held a long series of mid-level official posts, and discharged his duties adequately but not outstandingly. Like the Eight Talents, the Seven Later Masters consisted mainly of southerners who sought to turn the tables on their southern confreres, reject Song models, and revive the more disciplined Han and Tang standards of the Seven Early Masters. As a program aimed at mobilizing a new generation of literary talents, however, this was fuzzy, and indeed Wang himself violated it by his half-hidden admiration for the Song writers Su Dongpo and Sima Guang.

There were two searing episodes in Wang's life, and these drew wide attention. The first involved the execution of his year-mate Yang Jisheng in 1555 for his harsh criticism of Chief Grand Secretary Yan Song and his arguably weak policy toward the Mongols. Wang went to great lengths trying to plead on Yang's behalf, and then assisting his widow with the funeral. (Yan Song executed another year-mate, Shen Lian, in 1557.) Then, worst of all, Wang's own father was executed in 1560 for his terrible performance when as civilian supreme commander he did nothing to stop Altan Khan's deep raid toward Beijing. Wang and his brother went to extreme emotional lengths in a vain effort to save their father. There followed a long gap in Wang's own career, which he spent at home writing and exerting his literary influence far and wide. But still, just what did all this mean?

Wang, the great literary mogul of his time, never focused on any one thing, but spread his interests everywhere. At home for seven years after his father's execution, he designed an elaborate garden in the current style in which he entertained his many visitors. Wang was at times overbearing, but he could be friendly, with an uncanny ability to make younger men feel important and exceptionally talented. Of these younger men, there were a series of groups: first came the "Latter Five," then the "Supplemental Five," then the "Extended Five," and finally the "Terminal Five." But he held these followers at loose rein, and could not stop them from drifting off. Wang Daokun (1525–1593), a year-mate and one of the first group, had a successful bureaucratic career fighting pirates alongside Qi Jiguang; then, after 1575, he left government, developed a rivalry with Wang Shizhen, and made a good living writing epitaphs, poems, plays, and various occasional pieces for rich merchants.

At home again from 1576 to 1588, Wang escaped an unhappy and dysfunctional family life by moving out and living in a temple in the charge of Tan Yangzi (Wang Daozhen, 1558–1580, no relation), a religious mystic who was the daughter of an important friend. A cultural conservative, Wang Shizhen bemoaned what he saw as the erosion of literary and other standards, and the encroachment of commercial values into too many aspects of life. His hatred for Yan Song was lifelong, and while he probably did not write the famous play *Cry of the Phoenix* (*Ming feng ji*), which pits a thoroughly evil Yan Song against the admirable hero Yang Jisheng, he certainly helped promote it. Nor was Wang a supporter of the powerful Chief Grand Secretary Zhang Juzheng, even though he and Zhang were year-mates. As both Yan Song and Zhang Juzheng took an appeasement line with respect to Altan Khan, it is more than likely that Wang Shizhen would have been a die-hard hawk on the issue were it not for the complicating matter of his father's sorry performance in 1559.

So again, what should one make of Wang Shizhen's life and career? In an epitaph, Wang's longtime neighbor and friend Wang Xijue (1534–1611, who was Tan Yangzi's father) ventured to compare his influence in the world of his time to that of Wang Yangming. "For a time," he wrote, "the reverence of the literati for him was much like that accorded Wang Bo'an [Wang Yangming], when he was engaged in discussion and study, except that [Wang Shizhen] had the greater impact on prevailing customs and tastes." Indeed, in hindsight, one can see that Wang Shizhen and others in his cohort occupied a span of time between the post-1579 fading of the Wang Yangming schools and the rise of the Donglin faction from 1604, an interlude lying between two different Confucianist movements, when literary men and their values edged to the front of the list of national literati preoccupations. But they couldn't stay there. Their literary agenda was programmatically weak and diffuse, and their ability to mobilize other people was limited. But what Peter Bol has characterized as a major literati shift away from a Confucian idealism that "validated ignorance about the world" toward an emphasis on esthetics and erudition was in fact a much broader phenomenon, not limited to Wang Shizhen.[13]

In fact, Wang Shizhen and his admirers were soon challenged and then replaced by a new generation and a new literary movement, the so-called

Jingling and Gongan schools, named after two counties, native places of the founders, located within forty miles of each other along the Yangzi River in present-day Hubei province. Tan Yuanzhen (c. 1585–1637) and Zhong Xing (d. 1637) of Jingling championed pre-Tang and early Tang models for poetry. In Gongan, Yuan Hongdao (1568–1610) and his two brothers preferred a much freer style. Both objected to the standards Wang Shizhen had set. While they lent their names to the schools, neither Jingling nor Gongan served as gathering-places for interested literati. Macheng county, some two hundred miles northeast of those places, was a beneficiary of the late Ming wave of commercial prosperity and did serve as such a center; noted literati outsiders, such as the iconoclast Li Zhi, as well as Yuan Hongdao and his brothers and many others visited or sojourned there. But unquestionably the cultural capital of late Ming China was Suzhou (books published by members of the Jingling and Gongan schools sold very well there). Nanjing came in a close second, with Beijing perhaps third.[14]

By the seventeenth century, however, no school, literary or ideological, could dominate the attention of the whole educated class, as the sixteenth-century Wang Yangming phenomenon had once come close to doing. The literati population had grown, and their cultural center, Suzhou, developed and radiated far and wide a complex mixture of things to do, to write about, to discuss, to enjoy. Commoners as well as elites were engaged. There were orchestras and specialists in this or that musical instrument. There were many artists, some of whom aimed at faithful representations of the real world, others fantasies of the mind. There was a proliferation of new dramas and plays, which, like the *Cry of the Phoenix*, might depict recent sensational political events. Other plays might be airy romances. Yet others were serious explorations of human emotions. Music and drama combined in new ways, both raucous and melodic. Rich landed elites, often officials or retired officials, gathered their own acting troupes, built elaborate gardens following ever-shifting garden fashions, and in them often staged dramas and operas and lantern festivals and a range of other lavish entertainments. Connoisseurs of art, antiques, and literature rivaled each other in snobbery and discriminating expertise. Forgers of art, antiques, and writing abounded. Books of every sort and genre were produced in every style and format, from cheap editions to elaborate deluxe versions featuring fine illustrations and color printing. Anthologies of older writing jostled with a large choice of new literature: novels, short stories, poetry of all kinds, and recent history.

The coda of the late Ming literati could be described as variations on one theme, which was the great buzzword in circulation at the time—*qing*. The word meant on the one hand something real or factual, while on the other it meant emotion, passion, love, or any strongly felt desire. Avid art collectors, book lovers, music lovers, and girl chasers were all human types ensnared in *qing*. But not just these things. *Qing* could infect any endeavor. The Dong-lin Confucian martyrs who went knowingly to their deaths protesting the eunuch Wei Zhongxian and his cohorts in the 1620s were prime examples of men showing passionate righteousness in their cause. The seventeenth-century literati who, when their dynasty collapsed in the 1640s, organized suicidal defenses of Jiading and other cities in southeast China, exhibited in extreme form this all-consuming passion as well.

There were those who protested this penchant, however. There were those who voiced strong disapproval of the luxury and vice and erosion of standards that commercialization and silver monetization and increased urbanization had brought on. Many of these cultural critics were non-degree holders who lived in Jiangnan, the Yangzi delta region of southeast China, late Ming China's richest part. He Liangjun (1506–1573), Fan Lian (b. 1540), Zhang Tao (fl. 1607), Li Shaowen (c. 1570–1623), and Wu Lüzhen (d. 1645) were prominent among the many who complained harshly about the prevalent snobbery, ostentation, luxury, and selfishness of the society they lived in. They looked nostalgically back to the simpler and more honest ways of the past. And a few, such as Guan Zhidao (1536–1608), a Suzhou native, even thought about remaking the whole political and social structure of China. This reminds us of the Ming foundation years, the last time intellectuals thought along such lines, when Liu Ji and Fang Xiaoru developed plans to remold state and society. But there was a big difference. Liu Ji's ideas strongly influenced the Ming founding. But Guan Zhidao, and after him such leading minds as Gu Yanwu (1613–1682) and Huang Zongxi (1610–1695), who also had ideas about what had gone wrong with Ming China, and plans to remedy that, got nowhere with their ideas, as they had no part whatever in the Qing founding.[15]

What does this picture of the literati tell us about the durability of Ming China? One negative clue, but a clue of paramount importance, was the absence of any kind of anti-regime thinking and organizing among them. Despite all the flaws of the ruling system that they saw, despite all their dis-satisfactions with Ming China's social mores, despite all the philosophical, religious, and literary rivalries that again and again emerged over the course of the Ming centuries, very few literati ever joined efforts with any of the unhappy and rebellious masses, who would have needed their intellectual and organizational skills to bring off a revolution, as happened in the Ming founding. No, Ming China clearly provided too grand and too comfortable a context for literati self-fulfillment. Many literati also took seriously Fan Zhongyan's teaching—that the realm was not the monopoly of the emperor and the high officials, but was something that each individual had to assume personal responsibility for. Ming China persisted because the best and the brightest were, on the whole, happy with it.

CHAPTER FIVE

~

Outlaws

There were extensive areas—whole regions even—in the broad blanket of Ming local government where its threads were thin and its control negligible. This was typically the case in the mountainous interstices between provinces. On occasion these places, north and south, burst into outlawry on a fairly large scale. The problem was addressed, large Ming armies were mobilized, and the administrative holes patched until the 1630s and 1640s, when major internal disorder coincided with a foreign relations disaster in the shape of Manchu aggression, which led to the Ming collapse, beginning in the fateful year 1644.

It is sometimes difficult to tell whether a given upheaval should be characterized as internal or external. Troubles involving non-Chinese societies along or near the frontiers might be listed under either rubric. The rebellion of Man Si in western Shaanxi in 1468–1469, discussed in chapter 1, is a case in point. There were also huge, persistent, but intermittent risings among the various non-Chinese peoples of Guizhou and Guangxi through much of the Ming period. These were not strictly speaking frontier wars, because the non-Chinese peoples in question lived in big enclaves well inside the administrative boundaries of Ming China proper. How great a threat these may have posed to Ming security overall is uncertain, although to leave them unsuppressed was perceived by some authorities in Beijing as an invitation to the further spread of anarchy with consequences that could not be foreseen. Troops were mobilized in the tens and even hundreds of thousands, most of them tribal fighters under centrally appointed Ming commanders. The number of Chinese troops used in these interethnic wars was actually rather small, as historian Zhao Yi (1727–1814) pointed out long ago.[1]

If ethnic Chinese troops had a small presence in the far southwest, they had a heavy one along the northern frontiers. Among these troops, rebellion broke out in the garrison city of Datong in 1524 and again in 1533. These were mutinies, and it was harsh commanders that provoked them. In 1524, 2,500 troops and their families refused to relocate to five small forts that had just been built in the exposed flat country some thirty miles north of Datong. The forts were a death trap. The soldiers murdered and dismembered their commanders and ran riot inside Datong. In response, the Jiajing emperor sent out an expedition to suppress the mutineers. By 1525, his policy of executing the ringleaders and pardoning everyone else succeeded in dividing the rioters and quelling the uprising. But mutiny broke out again in 1533, involving many of the same participants. The cause of the trouble this time was the refusal of the troops to dig a thirteen-mile-long trench along one side of the city, within a time limit of three days, so as to frustrate Mongol cavalry raids. The mutineers repeated what happened nine years earlier, killing their commander and seizing the city of Datong. They also joined their erstwhile Mongol enemy in raiding. This went on for several months. Some of the Ming authorities on the spot demanded the suppression of this mutiny and general riot with utter ferocity, with no less than a general massacre. Fear of such a massacre kept the riot inside the city alive. It is to Jiajing's credit that he insisted that nothing of the kind should take place. So this second mutiny ended by the same discriminating policy that had ended the first. Ringleaders were executed; everyone else was let go. There were other Ming army mutinies at other garrisons; the special danger with those at Datong was their proximity to the Mongolian frontier. But it was purely local grievances that prompted them; they were in no way rebellions against or overt challenges to Ming rule.[2]

There were only a few rebellions in Ming times that were headed by religious figures purveying messianic doctrines. (It was just such an outbreak, the Red Turban rebellions of 1351–1354, that had contributed to the collapse of Yuan rule in China.) A famous example of such a rising was that led by the sorceress and self-styled "Buddha-mother" Tang Saier, that blazed for a short time in the spring of 1420 and affected several localities in central Shandong province. She attracted several thousand followers, but aside from raiding, their overall purpose or strategy doesn't seem clear. But the Yongle emperor was not complacent about it. After some initial faltering, Ming forces quickly quashed the disturbance. Tang Saier disappeared. Despite an exhaustive search—several thousand Buddhist and Daoist nuns were rounded up for questioning—no trace of her was ever found.[3]

The only prominent affair that at all resembled this one broke out two centuries later and encompassed some of the same Shandong territory. One of its leaders boasted some of the same magical powers as had Tang Saier. Other leaders were religious sectarians with a wide-ranging missionary organization that reached even into the imperial palace and won followers among the eunuchs and palace ladies. Rich men made generous contributions. This might perhaps have played out as Luo Qing's Buddhist movement, or Lin Zhaoen's church, as related in chapter 4, but it gathered momentum too close to Beijing, and officialdom was suspicious of it. Repression or the fear of it appears to have occasioned their revolt, led by one Xu Hongru. The affair lasted for six months in 1622. It broke out when the boy-emperor Tianqi emperor ruled; when an emerging partisan battle involving the Donglin was taking place; when the large-scale She-An rebellion was going on in the far southwest; and when the Beijing region was in panic, due to the collapse of the dynasty's defenses in Manchuria, and the influx of a large number of refugees from that area. If unattended to, Xu Hongru's revolt might well have metamorphosed into a serious threat to the dynasty. But the rebels were not well armed, and the Ming civil and military authorities put it down with efficiency and dispatch, and one never senses that it produced more than a momentary tremor. (Ironically, the Ming would fatally mishandle an internal disorder that began a mere six years later elsewhere in north China.)[4]

Longer-lasting, and much more demanding of the Ming dynasty's military and administrative resources, were four upheavals based mainly in rural south China: in Zhejiang and Fujian, 1447–1451; Hubei and Shaanxi, 1465–1476; Sichuan, 1507–1514; and Jiangxi, 1511–1519. These affairs featured little or nothing in the way of religious orientations, and their political goals and organization were rudimentary at best. What were they all about?

It is clear there was a burst of population growth in south China once peace and order returned after the Ming founding in 1368. People, seeking livelihoods and escaping tax and labor service demands, began to move into unoccupied but marginal land, beyond the effective reach of local government, mainly mountainous territory lying between one province and another.

The uplands east of Jiangxi and west of Zhejiang and Fujian were the scene of the first big outbreak. In the mountains west of Fujian, an outlaw and adventurer named Deng Maoqi, wanted for murder back in his home county in Jiangxi, took to pillaging silver mines to be found in the mountains, but the pickings were poor (the depletion of China's own silver deposits made the country a huge sinkhole for world silver in the following century). So he and his gang turned to robbing merchant convoys and plundering Fujian villages. The owner of a silver smelter joined him. The gang grew large. Deng styled himself "King of Fujian." He staged big raids on some of Fujian's principal administrative centers and, in so doing, attracted Beijing's attention. Forces from various parts were mustered into action. Some of Deng's lieutenants betrayed him. Deng himself was killed in action in April 1449. His nephew succeeded him, but mutual suspicions among the outlaws did them in, and the nephew was caught a month later, transported to Beijing, and there beheaded. Thus ended one outbreak.

In Zhejiang province meanwhile, another outlaw, this one named Ye Zongliu, a native of Qingyang county in Zhejiang, also turned from robbing silver mines to raiding villages and county seats in Zhejiang and in Fujian as well. Ye was killed in action late in 1448, but his successors continued to battle the Ming armies until the last of them was defeated in 1451.

One important key to understanding this violence as a crisis of law and order and not, say, a class war waged by the underprivileged or a failed attempt to overthrow the Ming dynasty, is that the authorities set up five new counties in the mountainous border regions of Zhejiang and Fujian once the suppression of the outlaws was over. Generally peaceful conditions reigned thereafter. Obviously, there were enough people in those regions to create a base adequate for the support of so many new units of local government. At no time did Beijing ever undertake to create new administrative centers lightly.[5]

The largest blank on the administrative map of interior China was the Austria-sized mountain region along the seams where three provinces joined: northern Huguang (today's Hubei), Henan, and Shaanxi. Because it lay beyond all government control, Ming authorities from the beginning of the dynasty declared it off-limits and forbade anyone to go in. But already by 1437, population pressure proved too intense, especially in times of famine in north China, when swarms of refugees entered to avail themselves of the wild foods of the mountains, rivers, and ravines. And there was vacant land that they could farm. Inevitably, in the absence of state-imposed security, the refugees fell under the control of outlaws, the first such being Liu Tong, known as "Thousand-Catty Liu," in recognition of his great physical strength. In 1465, Liu and several others established a primitive regime, with Liu as "King of Han" with a Buddhist temple for headquarters and several tens of thousands of fighters. They would emerge periodically from the mountains to plunder settled territory. Beijing took note and launched a major campaign in difficult terrain. The Ming armies conducted a mass slaughter. Liu Tong was captured alive in 1466 and sent to Beijing, where he was beheaded. The rest of his outfit was destroyed a few months later.

But then already in 1470 another rebellion took place in the same region. Drought and famine drove nearly a million refugees into the wilderness, and another Henan outlaw, this one known as Liu "Huzi" ("The Beard"), organized a predatory regime similar to that Liu Tong had led earlier. Beijing ordered up another large campaign to suppress it. This action accomplished its purpose late in 1471, with Liu Huzi captured and sent to Beijing for execution. But again the normal care taken to separate leaders from their hapless and pardonable followers was not taken. The censorial officials took note. They charged Xiang Zhong (1421–1502), the leading civil official (who had just had a big part in suppressing the rebellion of Man Si in Gansu), with having allowed a sickening massacre of innocent refugees who were good people until misfortune drove them from their farms, plots of land their ancestors had handed down to them. Plus Xiang countenanced a death march for many others, as the refugees who escaped massacre were forced to trudge off to garrisons in the extreme south of China. Some, however, insisted that Xiang, a brilliant fellow and a native of Jiaxing in Zhejiang, was charged unfairly with these horrors.

The end was not yet in sight. In 1476, another famine drove yet another wave of refugees into the mountains. This time, Beijing was persuaded to lift the restriction on entry and try a different approach to the problem. A censorial official, Yuan Jie (1417–1477), a native of Yangcheng in Shanxi province, was put in charge of establishing a wholly new apparatus of local government in the mountains, adequate to the task of administering to all the refugees who wished to stay and homestead in the once forbidden zone. Seven new counties were created in Henan, Shaanxi, and Hubei. A new prefecture, Yunyang, was set up on the upper Han River, where a military guards unit was posted, as well as a branch censorial office with supervisory responsibility over the lands of the three provinces that lay within the zone. After these measures were put in place, the region quieted down, and no more major upheavals occurred. Indeed, in the early 1640s, Yunyang put up a stout defense against the outlaw Li Zicheng (of whom more later).[6]

The Sichuan rebellions of 1507–1514 should never have persisted for seven long years. During that time, some half dozen roving outlaw formations rampaged across western Sichuan, south into Guizhou province, north into Shaanxi, and east into Yunyang, the new prefecture in Hubei that had just been set up a few decades before. These outlaws were not formidable opponents. The problem was that the Grand Coordinator Lin Jun (1452–1527) and the Supreme Commander Hong Zhong (1443–1523), civil officials, did not get along with each other. Plus the military officer corps was overloaded with the relatives and hangers-on of the Zhengde emperor's palace eunuchs. They were in the habit of declaring premature victories in order to reap the rewards and promotions. At length Peng Ze was put in sole charge of the suppression late in 1512. Peng was a tough, no-nonsense civil official, and native of the Lanzhou guards community in westernmost Shaanxi (nowadays Gansu province). By early 1514, he finished the job. Because this suppression was not followed by the creation of new county units, neither the causes of the outlawry nor the consequences of its destruction are wholly clear.[7]

In a study published in 1991, James W. Tong found in Ming official sources 630 instances of violence, most of it small-scale, that racked 1,097 counties during Ming times. He understated the case, as he omitted the violence-prone provinces of Sichuan, Guizhou, Yunnan, and Guangxi for which the data are insufficient or hard to use. He found that most of this violence affected south China, especially Fujian and Guangdong; that most of it took place during the second half of the Ming period; and that most of it is explicable as reactions to local crises of subsistence.[8]

The Zhengde reign (1505–1521) sat on the crest of a wave of rebellion that embroiled large parts of the country. Besides the Sichuan violence of 1507–1514, there was a raging situation in north China during the years 1509–1512, and turmoil aplenty in the province of Jiangxi and parts south during the years 1511–1519, culminating in the abortive revolt of Zhu Chenhao, Prince of Ning, in northern Jiangxi in 1519. A few remarks here about Jiangxi, then a look at the north China situation.

From 1511 to 1514, the fighting in Jiangxi took place mainly in the north of the province. Five different outlaw movements that based themselves in mountain stockades had to be eliminated one at a time by Ming armies. They were assisted by "wolf troops" drawn from the minority populations of the far south and southwest. At the end of military operations, two new counties were created (Dongxiang and Wannian), after which things quieted, only to flare up again briefly in 1519, as many ex-outlaws were attracted to the Prince of Ning's banners.

A mountainous four-province area, where southern Jiangxi abutted Fujian, Guangdong, and Huguang, was for decades outlaw territory whose masters beat off Ming attacks until 1515, when Wang Yangming was appointed Grand Coordinator with undiluted authority to pacify the region.

There is no doubt but that Wang was the most extraordinary talent Ming China ever produced. Not only was he an untiring and charismatic teacher and propagandist for his activist interpretation of Neo-Confucian doctrine, but he also showed an eagerness to exercise power in ways that were well thought out and productive of results. In his youth (and Wang was the son of a very successful scholar-official), he showed an interest in archery and frontier military matters, and as an official in his own right in 1510, he served half a year as magistrate of Luling county in central Jiangxi, during which time he was able not only to teach and discuss his philosophy, but also set in motion a reform of local security arrangements. Promoted to positions in Beijing and the secondary capital of Nanjing, his duties bored him, and he craved something more challenging. The Beijing Minister of War, Wang Qiong (1459–1532), an outstanding administrator himself, strongly recommended Wang Yangming's appointment as Grand Coordinator for southern Jiangxi.

Suffice it to say that Wang Yangming there became a virtual whirlwind of activity, establishing local security organs, recruiting and organizing an army of local men (avoiding the use of non-Chinese "wolf troops"), directing military operations against outlaw bases in the mountains, and then devising postwar settlements. Wang preferred cajolery and negotiation when dealing with outlaws; violence was always his last resort. The whole operation, involving tens of thousands of troops, was successfully completed in 1519. Two new counties were created. It was an outstanding achievement. (After his decisive defeat of the Prince of Ning, Wang would lead yet one more pacification campaign, this one in 1528 in Guangxi and Guizhou provinces, a region he was familiar with from his exile there years earlier. Aware that the non-Chinese rebels had been provoked by aggressive Chinese settlers, he sought to remedy the difficulty by striking an accord between the native *tusi* [chieftainships] and Ming Chinese administration.)

Historian Gao Dai (*jinshi* 1550) approved Wang Yangming's idea that negotiating with bandits with a view to arranging their peaceful surrender, pardon, and resettlement is workable only for followers sincere in their agreement to turn a new leaf; for hardened leaders, whose promises, if offered, are probably deceitful, violence must be used. In an astute comment on the dynamic of the situation, Gao Dai noted that the Jiangxi outbreaks were at the outset made worse by local officials who tried to avoid trouble by assuaging the outlaws, an approach which only encouraged more young men to become outlaws and "nest like bees and swarm like ants," and thus become very hard to eradicate. Following this growth of outlawry, the Ming authorities should have begun to divide leaders from followers, and offer surrender terms to the latter, but instead they turned to indiscriminate slaughter, which was completely useless, since it was mainly followers who got killed, rarely the leaders. The local officials, he conceded, early on probably had to do as they did, for lack of military resources sufficient to defeat the outlaws and restore law and order.[9]

The coalescence of many local bandit groups in Sichuan and Jiangxi and their growth into regional threats during Zhengde's time on the throne (1505–1521) looked dangerous, but the leaders of these groups never achieved much in the way of coherent organization or careful planning, which is one major reason why it proved possible for Ming government eventually to destroy them. A third regional congeries of outlaw activities, this in the years 1509–1512, was much more ominous, because it was centered in the northern metropolitan province (nowadays Hebei), and from there spilled southward into Shandong and Henan provinces and cut off the Grand Canal lifeline from south China to Beijing. These were "roving bandits" (*liu zei*), not as elsewhere occupying fixed mountain bases, owing to the flatness of the north China countryside. Ming-era commentators point out that for a century or more, since the Yongle wars of the early fifteenth century, there had been no major outbreaks of violence in this region, and so it was unprepared for trouble. Its prefectural and county seats were unwalled and undefended and so served as a sort of open smorgasbord of resources for raiders whenever they might appear.

When the raiders did appear, it was up to the magistrates to respond. Some did. Xu Kui (1484–1519), twenty-seven-year-old magistrate of Leling county in Shandong, got the local men to build a wall around the county seat, a job that took a month; then he had the people who lived inside put up high walls around their homes, with front gates wide enough to allow passage for only one person at a time and a strong young son to guard it with a sword. All the other boys he drilled as a militia and set up in ambushes in the interior alleys. When the raiders came, Xu gave a flag signal, and the boys waiting in ambush sprang into action. Unable to fight back or set fires, the raiders were all trapped and killed. Thereafter, roving bands avoided Leling. But this was an exceptional case. (Xu's talent impressed his superiors, and he was promoted, but his promising career ended a few years later when, as Surveillance Vice Commissioner in Jiangxi, he was killed in the rebellion of the Prince of Ning.)

There were two different aggregations of north China marauders. One was led by a certain Liu San as chief commander, with the assistance of Zhao Sui (also known as Zhao Fengzi, or "Madman Zhao"). Madman Zhao was an interesting fellow. He was a onetime government Confucian student (*shengyuan*) of Wenan county, sixty miles south of Beijing. He is described as a swashbuckling braggart. Marauders seized Zhao's wife and children and, using them as hostages, persuaded Zhao to join them. So Zhao Sui joined, as did his two brothers. By 1512, allies of this gang, led by Liu San, began organizing themselves and imposing discipline on their fighters. Under Zhao Sui's tutelage apparently, these marauders took on a political posture, as the righteous avengers of that party at court that had been cruelly crushed by eunuch dictator Liu Jin in 1506. This was a crowd-pleasing stance, and safe, because Liu Jin had been put to death two years earlier. The group did not venture to declare a new dynasty.

The other aggregation, loosely connected to Liu San's, was headed by two brothers from a military household in Bazhou, fifty miles south of Beijing. Liu Liu (Liu "Six") and Liu Qi (Liu "Seven") were denizens of a social world that had close ties with local men who were palace eunuchs (but not with Liu Jin, who was from Shanxi) and with a criminal underworld that conducted robberies and paid bribes to their contacts inside the Forbidden City. The Liu brothers formed a triumvirate of sorts with their comrade Qi Yanming, a felon whom they sprang from prison. It was they who kidnapped Zhao Sui's family. But the Liu brothers and Qi Yanming mostly rampaged separately from the group led by Liu San and Zhao Sui.

Beijing ordered troops to suppress these outlaws as early as 1509, but the marauders' strategy frustrated them. The hard core of leaders would force untrained youths recently recruited or shanghaied to face the Ming armies. The youths would take heavy casualties but hold off the armies long enough for the hard core to escape. The Ming armies stationed in the capital region were themselves poorly trained, and their commanders corrupt. They were susceptible to the outlaws' bribes and would also lodge spurious claims for rewards and promotions. So for three years the outlaws faced little in the way of serious resistance and freely raided and plundered large stretches of present-day Hebei, Shandong, and Henan provinces. Their main objective was to acquire horses, silver, and new recruits. They did not try to hold cities or occupy and defend territory.

What turned the tide was Zhengde's controversial decision to ignore the heated objections of Grand Secretary Li Dongyang and much of the rest of Ming bureaucracy, and bring about an interesting switch of military units— sending the hapless troops of the capital region to the northern frontiers and bringing the trained troops of the northern frontiers down to north China to take on the job of defeating the two major groups of marauders, which were growing ever larger and would probably soon be able to place a complete stranglehold on Beijing and precipitate a major civil war if not topple the Ming dynasty altogether. Historian Gao Dai thought the latter a definite possibility, had the outlaws been better organized and led. (It was in connection with bringing down the frontier troops that cavalry commander Jiang Bin, from the garrison city of Xuanfu, came to the Zhengde emperor's attention and became his closest companion, a sort of replacement for Liu Jin, for the remainder of the Zhengde reign period.)

The north China outlaws were no match for the experienced frontier armies. Beijing appointed an efficient and effective civilian commander: Peng Ze, who suppressed the main groups after a four months' campaign in 1512 and would go on to put down the disturbance in Sichuan two years later. As representative of the military, earl Qiu Yue (1465–1521), a onetime common soldier from Gansu who was adopted into a hereditary officer's family, performed admirably. The eunuch participant, Lu Yin, was ineffective. Some of the fighting was fierce and took place along the Yangzi River. Liu Qi and Qi Yanming met their end on October 31, 1512. Liu Liu was killed a bit earlier. Liu San and Zhao Sui also met their ends earlier, in the summer of 1512; Liu San fell in battle, but Zhao disguised himself as a Buddhist monk and hoped to flee south to Jiangxi province and join the outlaws who were active there. Unfortunately for him, soldiers responding to a wanted notice spotted him in a restaurant in a village near Wuchang in present-day Hubei province. He was arrested and transported to Beijing and there executed.

Zhengde officially declared the trouble over in late October 1512, when he issued rewards and promotions.[10]

～

As stated earlier, it was the ultimate nightmare of metastasizing internal rebellions coinciding with the external invasion of the Manchus that brought about the fall of the Ming dynasty in the mid-seventeenth century. The eventual leaders of the internal rebellions were Li Zicheng and his rival Zhang Xianzhong, both born in the year 1606 in villages a hundred miles apart from each other in the counties of Mizhi and Fushi, in the desolate loess country of northern Shaanxi province, not far from the Great Wall frontier. Both counties lay in Yan'an prefecture, the same remote region that served as the main base for Mao Zedong and the Communist guerrillas in the 1930s and 1940s.[11]

Ming China was so large that there was scarcely a time during its 276-year existence that violence requiring a military response was not taking place somewhere along the frontiers or in the interior. But, as noted earlier, this violence tended to come in waves, peaks followed by long troughs of relative calm. Internal violence also seemed to alternate with frontier turmoil—thus the Zhengde era (1505–1521) featured internal trouble in the rural areas of Sichuan, Jiangxi, and Hebei but relatively peaceful conditions along the frontiers. By contrast, the Jiajing era (1522–1566) enjoyed calm inside the country while war broke out along the northern and maritime frontiers. In the Wanli era (1573–1620), the maritime and northern frontier zones quieted down, the interior mostly remained calm, and frontier war shifted to new spots: the Bozhou campaign on the southwestern frontier in 1600; the short war in 1592 in Ningxia on the northwestern frontier; and the Korean interventions of 1592–1598. So the outbreak of rural violence inside China after 1628, the largest Ming China ever suffered, ended a century-long respite. It is, however, a surprising fact that the geographical launching site for this new round of violence was the northern provinces of Shaanxi and Shanxi, which had never been so involved before.

The disorders that got under way in 1628 lasted for the sixteen years that remained to the Ming, and on into early Qing times. Qing forces killed Li Zicheng in Tongshan county (south of Wuchang, in present-day Hubei province) in the late spring of 1645, and caught and killed Zhang Xianzhong in Xichong county in central Sichuan early in 1646. Remnants of their rebel armies escaped to south China and fought on through the 1660s. From beginning to end, this was one of the longest and most destructive human disasters China had ever undergone. (Perhaps the post-Han wars or the turmoil of the fourth to sixth centuries surpass it; the Mongol invasion of the early thirteenth-century challenges it as well, but those disasters were perpetrated mainly by invaders from the steppes, not so much by internal rebels.)[12]

An unfortunate combination of factors precipitated the late Ming upheavals. A list of them would have to include persistent drought, crop failures, and famine as well as troop mutinies and desertions—problems endemic along the extreme northwestern edge of China, normally within the capacity of government to alleviate and surmount. But by the 1620s, Beijing was having a fiscal crisis, and it had to debase the copper coinage and impose a series of tax surcharges in order to meet the soaring costs of frontier wars in the southwest and in Manchuria. The fighting in Manchuria, which was not going well, nor showing signs of ending anytime soon, was clearly Beijing's main preoccupation. Outlawry in Shaanxi and Shanxi was for a while of secondary concern. Manpower and resources were needed elsewhere.

By 1629, however, disturbing reports of a half dozen risings in Shaanxi involving local famine refugees and cavalry troops who had deserted from the Manchurian front reached the young and conscientious Chongzhen emperor. He decided the situation needed attention. He assigned a position no one at the time wanted, that of civilian supreme commander in the Shaanxi frontier region, to one Yang He (died in exile, ca. 1635). It was not a bad choice. Yang He, a native of Wuling in southern Huguang province (nowadays Hunan), achieved his *jinshi* degree in 1604, and had already had experience with frontier matters in Guizhou and Manchuria, and had written in 1628 a widely read memorial describing what he took to be a national crisis of exhaustion of human will as well as material resources. The troubles in Shaanxi he diagnosed as simply a rising of famine victims whom local officials had failed to relieve. Yang insisted that all that needed doing was to soothe the mutinous troops, and the expenditures for that would be minimal. That was what Chongzhen needed to hear, and so he appointed Yang He. It made sense.

But Yang He seriously underestimated the seriousness of the situation. The year 1630 found Yang He out in the field in Shaanxi overseeing operations. Immediately he was faced with Ming troop mutineers. Fearing punishment, the mutineers joined forces with local outlaws. Yang needed help from Beijing to handle this, but none was forthcoming. On his own authority, he negotiated with the mutineers and issued them all certificates of amnesty; but the outlaws continued to raid, and there was little Yang could do about it. The disorders spread east into Shanxi province. Borrowing a page from Wang Yangming, perhaps, Yang He set up an impressive ceremony for some surrendered outlaws and got them to agree to return either to their military units or to their farms and shout *wansui*! in honor of the emperor, in return for which he granted them all pardons. However, unlike Wang Yangming, Yang did not command credible military force, and the outlaws knew that. So his policy of conciliation, and his personal assets of sincerity and of courage in conferring alone and unarmed with some of the outlaw leaders, in the end came to naught. In 1631, censors impeached Yang for his failure. Chongzhen angrily sent him into exile. Now what?[13]

Chongzhen appointed as Yang He's replacement a very capable civil official—Hong Chengchou (1593–1665), a native of Quanzhou prefecture in Fujian province. Policy shifted from reliance on conciliation to an insistence on dealing with the outlaws from a position of strength. The outlaws were not a popular force. Often they had to recruit by harsh means, cutting off the hair of the unwilling so as to mark them off from the regular population and so discourage their escape. Hong distrusted and dealt severely with the outlaw leaders, but was willing to pardon followers. Meanwhile, he used the armed forces at his disposal to isolate and take down the five main Shaanxi outlaw gangs. By early 1634, he cleared Shaanxi of its thugs. However, remnants escaped into neighboring provinces: eastward into Shanxi, Henan, and the northern metropolitan region, and southward into Sichuan. And now what?[14]

The outlaws, now scattered, gained new recruits and learned to conduct cavalry raids while avoiding battling the Ming armies. Chongzhen yielded to pleas that the Ming enhance its suppression efforts, and so in 1635 he reluctantly granted Hong unlimited authority for six months to direct a multi-provincial operation against an outlaw movement that had by now swollen to the hundreds of thousands. The outlaws outnumbered the hapless Ming armies, which were fast becoming demoralized by their inability to score any victories, and so suffered mutinies and defections to the enemy side. Unconfirmed reports had it that early in 1635 thirteen big outlaw leaders had held a two-week gathering at Yingyang county (sometimes rendered as Rongyang) in northern Henan province just south of the Yellow River, and had agreed to coordinate their movements and share out the plunder. Li Zicheng, though not a main leader at the time, is said to have played a major part in securing that agreement. Zhang Xianzhong also is rumored to have attended, as one of the main leaders. (Despite Li's supposed peacemaking, he and Zhang would never get along.)

Thus Hong Chengchou was faced with a problem that could hardly be handled within the six months' time the emperor gave him. It did help that in October 1635 Chongzhen appointed another civil official, Lu Xiangsheng (1600–1638), a native of Yixing in the southern metropolitan province, to a position comparable to Hong's for northeast China, and ordered the two, Lu and Hong, to cooperate with each other in defeating the outlaws. Both were excellent choices. Lu was a superb and energetic commander. Training and logistics improved. The top outlaw leader, Gao Yingxiang (Li Zicheng's superior), fell to Hong's forces in central Shaanxi in the late summer of 1636. That blow dealt a temporary setback to the outlaws' capabilities. It seemed safe to reassign Lu to the northern frontier, where, unfortunately, Manchu troops killed him two years later.[15]

Meanwhile, Chongzhen made more moves to destroy the outlaws once and for all. In the summer of 1637, he appointed no less a figure than Yang Sichang (1588–1641), son of the disgraced Yang He, as Minister of War and grand strategist for the whole operation. Yang's plan, highly controversial, was to negotiate a temporary peace agreement with the Manchus so that the court's whole attention could focus on the internal problem. Early in 1638 the grand strategy was set in motion: the formation of a gigantic double-ringed circle of containment, involving ten different provincial armies, while a mobile striking force, 120,000 strong, under the overall command of Xiong Wencan, a civil official and *jinshi* of 1607, set forth from Yunyang (the prefecture created in northern Huguang in 1476) to engage and destroy all remaining outlaw concentrations. This was forecast to cost 2.8 million taels silver, of which amount most came from yet another special tax surcharge. The whole operation was supposed to take three months.

However, Xiong Wencan was a poor choice for the job. It is not clear just where he originally came from, but he eventually got himself registered in Qishui county in northern Huguang. He certainly had experience in dealing with rebels and outlaws, having arranged the surrender of the pirate Zheng Zhilong in 1628, and then getting Zheng to turn on and defeat the pirate Liu Xiang in 1635. But Xiong was not a charismatic fighter like Lu Xiangsheng. He was a dealmaker and negotiator, a sort of sleazy Yang He, who preferred sweet talk and bribery to violence in handling outlaw leaders. And now here, instead of crushing the outlaws as he was expected to do, he changed the plans and persuaded them to surrender. (For some reason, Chongzhen and Yang Sichang endorsed that change of plan.) Xiong then let the outlaws settle together in one area, as though they had suddenly become sincere Ming loyalists. Some of them were not. Zhang Xianzhong resumed raiding in the early summer of 1639.

Meanwhile, key units of the Ming army had to be shifted from the interior war in order to defend Beijing against Manchu incursions. Hong Chengchou and his men, who had all but destroyed Li Zicheng, were among them. Thus the outlawry, so nearly contained and defeated, roared back into life. Xiong Wencan was put under arrest, taken to Beijing, and executed. Yang Sichang volunteered to go to northern Huguang himself and assume supreme command again. Too late, forcible methods replaced negotiation as strategy. Zhang Xianzhong used hit-and-run tactics to outmaneuver Yang Sichang's pursuers in Sichuan, and in early 1641 he turned east to devastate northern Huguang. The other main outlaw leader, Li Zicheng, meanwhile seized the city of Luoyang in northern Henan. On April 10, 1641, in utter despair, Yang Sichang committed suicide. An ongoing effort to buy peace with the Manchus, conducted in secrecy on Chongzhen's orders, was exposed by accident, leading to such a furor of protest at court that the negotiation had to be canceled and the Minister of War who was involved in the policy, Chen Xinjia, executed. This was in the summer of 1642.

Captured in Manchuria on March 19, 1642, Hong Chengchou defected to the Manchu side. Sun Chuanting (1593–1643), who had cooperated effectively with Hong in the near destruction of Li Zicheng, was killed in a hopeless battle against him in Xi'an in 1643. From 1639 on, the revived outlaws assumed the initiative and inflicted defeat after defeat on the hapless Ming armies. The unraveling of the Ming was horrifying to behold. The collapse of the whole system was very near.[16]

Ming sources routinely treat outlaws with disdain, which makes them hard to learn about and understand. Likewise, every outlaw or rebel movement that took place in Ming times failed, and therefore none of them was ever able to produce an inner history or a narrative of their own. We have official sources only, which are hostile, and dwell on the Ming side of the story to the exclusion of any other perspective. This does not necessarily make them wrong, but it does make them incomplete. For the outlaw side, one has to rely on inference, or on chance remarks.

The two men who eventually rose to the top of the late Ming outlaw movements, and turned them into rebellions, were Zhang Xianzhong and Li Zicheng. Though never friendly, they were together responsible for inflicting ten years of slaughter, destruction, and mayhem on an enormous scale over parts of seven already outlaw-troubled provinces of mostly north China: Shaanxi, Shanxi, Henan, northern Huguang (now Hubei), the northern part of the southern metropolitan region (now Anhui), the northern metropolitan region (now Hebei), and Sichuan. Can anything reliable be learned about what kinds of men these were?

A story about Zhang Xianzhong, probably apocryphal, is nonetheless interesting. As a boy, the story goes, he accompanied his father, a butcher and wood dealer, with a cartload of jujube wood on an eight-hundred-mile trip from northern Shaanxi south to Neijiang, a county in Sichuan, not far from the Yangzi River. In Neijiang, their donkey defecated in front of the stone gateway leading to the residence of some member of the local elite. A servant came out, scolded Zhang's father and whipped him, and made him remove the mess with his bare hands. Young Zhang Xianzhong witnessed this in anger, but dared say nothing. This story might be true in the sense that something of the sort happened in Zhang's childhood that prompted his lifelong hatreds and the mass murders he later conducted as rebel leader, especially in Sichuan. Was he avenging his father's humiliation?[17]

The early stages of Zhang's career seem to be these: expulsion from school for assaulting a classmate; ejection from his family for his misbehavior, apparently; a job as a policeman in Yan'an prefecture; then loss of the job when the position was eliminated. Tall, swaggering, and intimidating, Zhang next took up arms as a frontier soldier and did well, fighting and accumulating livestock, but was nearly executed as a result of some complicated accusations laid against him. Dismissed from the army, Zhang gathered a following and turned outlaw, as many other renegades and military deserters were then doing. This would have been 1630. Zhang and his men joined first one, then another outlaw leader. He surrendered to Supreme Commander Hong Chengchou sometime late in 1631, then followed Gao Yingxiang in turning outlaw again. By late 1632, he had ravaged Shanxi, Henan, Anhui (the northern part of the southern metropolitan region), Huguang, and Shaanxi.[18]

From this point, the historical record about Zhang becomes much fuller. What needs focusing on here, however, is not the seesawing, month-by-month battle reports, but the specific issue of the moves Zhang made to turn an aimless outlawry into a serious-minded rebellion—an organized effort to create an independent, post-Ming government, with himself as ruler of it.

The first such move came in northern Huguang (presently northern Hubei province) in 1642, when he captured the prefectural city of Wuchang, which he renamed Tianshou fu ("Heaven-conferred prefecture"). Zhang took the title Da Xi Wang ("King of the Great West"). He eliminated the local Ming prince of Chu by having him drowned in the Yangzi, butchered all the other Zhu clansmen, seized the princely residence, and made it his palace. A million or so taels silver was gathered from somewhere and hauled in by the cartload. Banners at all the city gates provided the essential propaganda:

"Heaven gives, the people adhere"; "We welcome and employ worthy *shi* [members of the educated class]"; "Peace in the realm"; and "We defend the eight points of the compass." Military and civil organs of government were set up, following the familiar Ming pattern. Civil service examinations were arranged. Thirty men were awarded the *jinshi* degree and appointed as magistrates to the twenty-one counties and subprefectures that Zhang controlled. Forty-eight other examinees were appointed to subordinate civil posts.

Li Zicheng held Xiangyang prefecture, just north of Zhang's domain. He sent Zhang a threatening message. Zhang proffered tribute. Then in the late summer of 1643, a massive Ming assault from downriver recaptured Wuchang amid indescribable slaughter, and forced Zhang and his Great Western regime to flee.

Looking for a new home, Zhang and his forces rampaged through southern Huguang (now Hunan) and Jiangxi provinces, as far south as northern Guangdong in the autumn of 1643. Zhang then chose Changsha prefecture in Hunan as the site for his new capital. There he began setting up a civilian administrative apparatus along the same lines he'd used in Hubei. Most of the counties and prefectures in Hunan and Jiangxi, terrorized by Zhang's credible threats of massacre and attracted by his offers of tax relief, capitulated to him without struggle. A huge realm in south central China was his. Then, in a strange decision, he abandoned it all in early 1644. He and his regime migrated west up the Yangzi and into Sichuan province. Ming forces then recaptured Hunan and Jiangxi without difficulty.[19]

Zhang and his enormous army captured the prefecture of Chongqing in Sichuan in July 1644, and Chengdu two months later. He made Chengdu his imperial capital. Much of the rest of Sichuan fell soon after. Most of the frontier chieftaincies (*tusi*) surrendered in return for payoffs and tax remissions. A few refused to submit. One was the Shizhu Chieftaincy, led by a woman, known to history by her Chinese name, Qiu Liangyu. Zhang left her alone.

Zhang's unforced and seemingly inexplicable abandonment of Hunan and Jiangxi may have been prompted by a policy bind. On the one hand, he had an army numbering in the hundreds of thousands that had somehow to be funded and fed. On the other hand, he had issued tax remissions across the board to every locality that had put up no resistance to him. It appears, therefore, that he abandoned the whole region because he couldn't afford to stay there.

In Sichuan, Zhang's policies have been labeled as "genocidal." That is surely the wrong word, if by "genocidal" one means a deliberate effort to destroy a whole nation or class. This third try at establishing a regime was, however, brutal beyond doubt. Zhang imposed a heavy police presence in

Sichuan, and his minions were mercilessly cruel to anyone suspected of the slightest infractions. Was he thinking of his father's humiliation years before? Whatever the case, his Great Western empire was heavily military and only lightly civilian, and he was not secure in it. While he was in the act of making grandiose plans for using Sichuan as a launching site for conquest everywhere, independent outlaws and warlords, some of them loosely associated with the Southern Ming resistance, challenged his frontiers, "hacking away, month after month, at the periphery of his domain," as James B. Parsons describes it. Zhang lost the city of Chongqing to such hacking in 1645. Defections and mutinies and plots, some real, some suspected, elicited ever more murderous responses from Zhang. By 1646, Sichuan was a hopeless ruin. True to form, Zhang tried to evacuate it and, for the fourth time, set up a new base somewhere else; it is not clear where. He moved as far as Xichong, some 125 miles east of Chengdu, and there Manchu forces killed him, probably on January 2, 1647.[20]

Zhang had no sons of his own. Two adopted sons, local compatriots from northern Shaanxi, had served him well and loyally for years as top-ranking generals. After Zhang's death, both moved south with their troops and joined the Southern Ming cause. One of them, Sun Kewang, defeated by his adoptive brother and rival, Li Dingguo, in battle in 1657, defected to the Manchu Qing and died peacefully, well rewarded, in Beijing in 1660. (The Jesuit missionary Gabriel de Magalhães knew Sun in Sichuan and had a high opinion of him.) Li Dingguo remained loyal to the Ming to the very end, dying of sickness in Burma in 1662, just after the Southern Ming court's extinction.[21]

So ended the Great Western regime. Why, in hindsight, did it never stand a chance to supplant the Ming and rule China? Zhang Xianzhong's story invites comparison with that of the Ming founder, Zhu Yuanzhang. Zhang Xianzhong did not lack for vigor and prowess, and he seems to compare well with the Ming founder in his ability to attract capable generals and others to his banner. Neither man was educated, but Zhang never understood that deficiency well enough to seek the advice of those who were well educated. More to the point, he had no proclivity, as the Ming founder did, to discriminate among advisors, bypass the more limited ones, and find the more capable. Zhang had resources aplenty, but was intellectually adrift. If there were a Liu Ji out there, Zhang made no effort to find him. He did not know that he did not know how to found a dynasty. Unlike Zhu Yuanzhang, who soon left the millenarian White Lotus Buddhism of his early rebel days far behind him, Zhang Xianzhong was never able to outgrow the bloody-minded ruffianism of his youth.[22]

～

Li Zicheng did slightly better than Zhang did at dynasty founding. Li came from a peasant village located some sixty miles west of the Mizhi county seat in northern Shaanxi province. His family had been one of moderate means, not poor, until the time of his grandfather and father, when it faced ruin due to the labor service requirements connected with providing horses for government use. Young Li had to seek a living as a hired shepherd and in an assortment of other jobs. Local government hired him as a post station attendant. Around 1630, Li and his co-workers lost their jobs when, during a severe famine, government eliminated them so as to ease the service burden on the distressed peasantry. Li, together with some friends and relatives, then joined a unit of the Ming army that was campaigning in western Shaanxi (Gansu province today). Sometime in 1631, it appears, Li and his group mutinied over a lack of supplies and returned east to lead a life of plunder and outlawry. Li placed himself under the command of Gao Yingxiang, to whom he may have been related, until Gao's death in 1636.[23]

We will not follow Li and the other outlaw gangs over the next several years, as the Ming armies under Hong Chengchou and Yang Sichang chased them and squeezed them and nearly extinguished them. In 1638, Li and Zhang Xianzhong met in Hubei and talked about merging their remnant forces, but they distrusted each other and failed to come to an agreement.

When the Ming was compelled to shift forces back to the Beijing region, the interior rebellions revived, and Zhang and Li emerged from hiding and both began to think about occupying territory rather than simply raiding it and seizing cities as well as rural areas. In the late winter of 1641, his army rapidly swelling with young famine refugees, Li moved east into Henan province and captured the city of Luoyang (Henan fu). There he murdered the unpopular Prince of Fu (Wanli's son by the notorious Lady Zheng), seized his fortune and large grain stores, and distributed it, or some of it, to the needy. This was a worrisome blow for the Ming court. (Simultaneously, Zhang Xianzhong took a major city, Xiangyang, in northern Huguang.)

Would Li base a regime in Luoyang, imperial capital several times in China's long past? No. From Luoyang, Li at once moved east to assault the Henan provincial capital, Kaifeng; but the resident Prince of Zhou liberally funded the defense, the defense was effective, and Li broke the siege after only six days. He captured and inflicted much slaughter on smaller places in the south central part of the province. He lost interest in Luoyang, and it soon reverted to Ming control.

In January 1642, Li attacked Kaifeng again. First he tried bombarding the walls with cannon fire. Then he tried mining the walls. Thousands of his men worked for a week digging thirty-six holes through 120 feet of wall. The defenders repelled these assaults, and after about a month Li's food supplies ran low and he ended the siege. He resumed raiding operations elsewhere until May 1642, when he made a third assault on Kaifeng, this time planning to take it down by starving out its defenders. Outside help was not available, yet Kaifeng refused to yield. Both the defenders and Li then tried using the Yellow River against each other—the defenders attempted to breach the dikes and wash away Li's army, while Li did the same to flood the city and destroy it. Li won. On October 8, 1642, Li's men cut the dikes, and a rain-swollen Yellow River burst through with a tremendous roar, flooding Kaifeng, drowning many thousands, completely wrecking the city, and causing many more thousands of casualties by way of exposure and starvation. Life and property losses were truly catastrophic.

What now? As of 1642, Li was still an outlaw and warrior who was trying to gain control over several other semi-independent warlords and their armies, and was therefore not yet in a position to give full attention to building administrative institutions and creating stability. So from the flooded ruin of Kaifeng he withdrew two hundred miles southwest to Xiangyang. There he murdered several allies and incorporated their fighters, started building a palace and casting coin, made some high-level civil appointments, and promoted himself from generalissimo to king. After half a year, however, neither Li nor his advisors thought Hubei would do as a permanent home base; and after considering other options, they decided their best bet was to evacuate Hubei and reoccupy familiar territory in Shaanxi and Shanxi and make that region a base for mounting a direct assault on Beijing. So in the late summer of 1643, the regime took to the road. Li's army defeated a Ming force under Sun Chuanting in November of that year, battled its way into the Wei River valley of southern Shaanxi, and seized the city of Xi'an. Here, Li resumed the dynasty-founding efforts he'd begun at Xiangyang. He now announced a dynastic name ("Great Shun"), held civil service examinations, appointed the graduates as local magistrates, ennobled his ancestors, created a military nobility, issued a calendar, and cast a special coinage. Again, he did not bother to consolidate further. Almost immediately (in January 1644), he started his ultimately successful march on Beijing.

That march, about six hundred straight-line miles northeast across Shanxi from Xi'an, took four months. Parsons remarks that it was as much a triumphal procession as a military campaign, in that Li's propaganda was effective and Ming resistance minimal. Great Wall frontier garrisons at Datong and

Xuanfu capitulated easily. Beijing was in desperate straits. It had run out of funds and began demanding silver contributions from everyone. Commander Wu Sangui and others did not obey commands to rush to the capital's defense. The Chongzhen emperor then handed the task over to the palace eunuchs. Li reached Beijing on April 23, 1644, organized a siege, and offered terms to Chongzhen: he would settle for less than the imperial throne; a title, regional control over northwest China, and a million taels silver would do. Chongzhen refused to negotiate. On April 25, he and a eunuch companion committed suicide.

For forty days, from April 25 to June 6, 1644, Li Zicheng's Great Shun dynasty ruled north China, more or less. This was in a way a historic triumph, a rise of outlawry to serious power, such as to rival the Huang Chao rebellion of 875–884. But Li now identified himself with the Tang rulers, with whom he shared the Li surname, not with Huang Chao. As ruler, sitting where once the Ming emperors had sat, Li comported himself with modesty and simplicity. He had some good ideas for reforming social and economic abuses. As he had done in Xi'an, so in Beijing too he targeted well-off people for revenues (collecting or extorting an estimated seventy million taels from them) and terminated tax exemptions for members of the official class and their families. He held another civil service exam and assigned those who passed to local magistracies. He expelled thousands of eunuchs from the Forbidden City. He gave Chongzhen, whose corpse was found a few days later, a dignified burial, and conferred a title on his heir apparent.

Most of the two thousand or so Ming officials on duty in Beijing, as well as those serving elsewhere in north China, were willing to submit and swear loyalty to the Great Shun. Li made serious efforts to discipline his troops when they first entered Beijing, and he had some success in preventing looting and other misbehavior. The Shun regime, in short, was giving every sign that it had outgrown its outlaw origins and was conducting itself as a legitimate dynasty with good policies and an earnest commitment to administrative order and rationality. But it lasted only forty days. Something was terribly wrong with it, obviously.

This was no rerun of the story of Ming Taizu's rise to power in the 1360s, even though the Ming founder and his military, all of them lower-class, unlettered natives of the war-racked Huai region of north central China, had, like Li and his followers from northern Shaanxi, emigrated far from home to base themselves elsewhere. How does one explain the puzzle of the precipitous Shun collapse?

Some systemic flaws predated the Shun takeover of Beijing. Li never managed to attract literati of high ability and empire-wide renown to his cause. After his strategic shift from roving outlawry to the capture of big cities, he nowhere did anything to revive the rural economy. He was always on the move. And his management of his top military people was faulty. He murdered some, thereby creating resentments among the followers. Other of his generals continued to act semi-independently, following outlaw tradition. Thus as Li made moves in Beijing to assume autocratic authority in the mold of an emperor, one of his top generals, Liu Zongmin, refused to knuckle under, and conducted on his own authority an erratic, sadistic, and brutal round-up, torture, extortion, and murder of ex-Ming officials. Meanwhile, his own troops broke discipline and ran amok in the city of Beijing, breaking into homes, looting, raping, and torching at will. These horrors quickly negated what popular support the Shun had begun to enjoy.

So with shaky control of a ravaged countryside, with a military machine he did not fully control, and with a confused and terrorized urban population turning against him, Li had to focus attention on the Manchu problem to the northeast. The Ming general in charge there was Liaodong native Wu Sangui (1612–1678). His base was Ningyuan, on the sea about seventy-five miles northeast of Shanhaiguan, a key entry point at the eastern extremity of the Great Wall. Responding tardily to the Chongzhen emperor's cry to come help defend Beijing, Wu and his army had come as far as Shanhaiguan when the news reached him that Beijing had fallen. He also heard that Li's men had made a hostage of his father, a retired military man, and were extorting silver from him. Li sent an envoy to Wu, inviting him to surrender to the Shun cause. Wu declined to do so. So on May 18, Li personally led an army out of Beijing to attack Wu. Many of Li's men, meanwhile, loaded with loot, were drifting back to their home territory in Shaanxi. Faced with attack, Wu aligned himself with his erstwhile enemy, the Manchu Dorgon, acting as regent for the child emperor Shunzhi and camped near Shanhaiguan. On May 27, their armies joined and demolished Li's, which had little stomach for the fight. Li and his defeated troops straggled back to Beijing and there conducted a mad orgy of looting and arson. Li himself flew into a paroxysm of vengeance. He murdered thirty-eight members of Wu Sangui's family and hung the severed head of Wu's father over one of Beijing's walls. Li had, prudently perhaps, never gone so far as to declare himself emperor of his Shun dynasty, only king. But on June 3, with everything lost, he declared himself emperor. Why not? The next day, June 4, he and his remaining followers, reverting to their familiar outlawry, evacuated Beijing for parts west.

So ended the Shun. Its existence, however, served an important function: the Manchu Qing entrance into Beijing on June 6 was justified by regent Dorgon in his public propaganda not as a blatant overthrow of Ming power, but as revenge on behalf of the Ming against the murderous outlaw regime of Li Zicheng, and as a beacon of hope for the restoration of Ming-style order and civilization to the beleaguered and brutalized people of Beijing and north China. That was not an empty promise. The Qing regime by now comprised many ethnic Chinese natives of Manchuria (like Wu Sangui) and Chinese officials who had defected earlier (like Hong Chengchou). It had already built a Ming-style machine of civil administration that was better organized than anything Li Zicheng or Zhang Xianzhong had been able to engineer. The Qing had serious flaws of its own, to be sure. And it would take them forty years to complete the conquest of China. It had taken the Ming founder, Taizu, less than half that time to accomplish the same.[24]

Large-scale internal rebellions inflicted severe damage on nearly every one of the great unified dynasties of China's past. One thinks of the upheavals that led to the end of the Former Han in the early years of the first century, and to the piecemeal collapse of the Later Han after 184. The Tang was knocked severely askew by the rebellions of the mid-eighth century, and then was destroyed altogether in the wake of those of the late ninth. Empire-wide rebellion was the indirect cause of the Yuan collapse after 1351. And the Qing barely survived the great rebellions of the mid-nineteenth century. Indeed, it might have collapsed then had the British, French, and Russians not preferred for the time being to keep it afloat. Had the Manchus chosen the same policy in the seventeenth century—that is, had they stayed in Manchuria and exploited the Ming from afar, then the Ming might well have survived the rebellions of Li Zicheng and Zhang Xianzhong, but with an institutional profile resembling that of the late Qing (or Later Han or late Tang)—in other words, a dynasty only in nominal control of China, with fiscal and other key powers in the hands of semi-autonomous regional authorities. It was out of such a compost heap of state breakdown that a rebel like the Ming founder arose in the mid-fourteenth century.

~

Notes

Chapter 1: Frontiers

1. Edward L. Farmer, *Zhu Yuanzhang and Early Ming Legislation* (Leiden: E. J. Brill, 1995), 120.

2. For Ming relations with Vietnam, I have relied upon Wang Gungwu, "Ming Foreign Relations: Southeast Asia," in *The Cambridge History of China: Volume 8: The Ming Dynasty, 1368–1644*, part 2, ed. Denis Twitchett and Frederick W. Mote (Cambridge: Cambridge University Press, 1998), 301–32; L. Carrington Goodrich and Chaoying Fang, eds., *Dictionary of Ming Biography* (New York: Columbia University Press, 2 vols., 1976), biographies of Chang Fu, Huang Fu, Lê Lợi, Lê Quí-ly, Mac Dang-dung; John C. Whitmore, "Chiao-chih and Neo-Confucianism: The Ming Attempt to Transform Vietnam," *Ming Studies* 4 (Spring 1977): 57–92; Chen Zilong, ed., *Huang Ming jingshi wenbian* (1638, reprint Taipei: Guolian tushu chuban youxian gongsi, 30 vols., 1968), 3:381 (a memorial by Zhang Fu).

3. For the *tusi* system generally, I consulted Gong Yin, *Zhongguo tusi zhidu* (Kunming: Yunnan minzu chubanshe, 1992).

4. For Luchuan, see John E. Herman, *Amid the Clouds and Mist: China's Colonization of Guizhou, 1200–1700* (Cambridge, Mass.: Harvard University Press, 2007), 86–87, 118–20, 144–45, 236; Goodrich and Fang, eds., *Dictionary*, biographies of Chen Yung-pin, Ts'ao Chi-hsiang, Wang Chi, Ssu-jen-fa; Zhang Tingyu, ed., *Ming shi* (1736; there are several modern versions, thus a citation just to chapter, ch., or Chinese *juan*, will suffice), ch. 162 (biography of Wang Ji); Chen Zilong, ed., *Huang Ming*, 4:94–97 (memorial by Liu Qiu).

5. For Bozhou, Goodrich and Fang, eds., *Dictionary*, biographies of Li Hua-lung, Yang Ying-lung, Kuo Tzu-chang, Liu T'ing; Chen Zilong, ed., *Huang Ming*, 26:160–73 (memorial by Li Hualong).

6. Herman, *Amid the Clouds and Mist*, 187; Gu Yingtai, Mingshi jishi benmo (1658, several modern versions), ch. 64.

7. Elliot Sperling, "The Szechwan-Tibet Frontier in the Fifteenth Century," *Ming Studies* 26 (Fall 1988): 37–55; Weirong Shen, "'Accommodating Barbarians from Afar': Political and Cultural Interactions between Ming China and Tibet," *Ming Studies* 56 (Fall 2007): 37–93; Goodrich and Fang, eds., *Dictionary*, biographies of Yon-tan-rgya-mts'o, Tsong-kha-pa, dGe-'dun-grub; Halima, dGe-dun-rgya-mts'o, bSod-nams-rgya-mts'o; Chen Zilong, ed., *Huang Ming*, 12:613–17 (memorial by Huo Tao); 23:271–74 (letter to Guo Huanyi from Zhang Siwei); 23:589–91 (memorial by Shen Shixing); 24:176–204 (Xu Yuantai reports); Zhang Tingyu, ed. *Ming shi*, ch. 247 (biography of Li Yingxiang); ch. 311 (description of Songpan).

8. Gao Dai, *Hongyou lu* (1557, reprint Taipei, 1977), 1196; Goodrich and Fang, eds., *Dictionary*, biographies of Mao Chung and Hsiang Chung; Gu Yingtai, *Mingshi jishi benmo*, ch. 41.

9. Arthur Waldron, *The Great Wall of China: From History to Myth* (Cambridge: Cambridge University Press, 1990), 142; Beatrice Forbes Manz, *The Rise and Rule of Tamerlane* (Cambridge: Cambridge University Press, 1989), 73, 186n27; Morris Rossabi, "Cheng Ho and Timur: Any Relation?" *Oriens Extremus*, 20 (1973): 129–36; Rossabi, "Two Ming Envoys to Inner Asia," *T'oung Pao* 62 (1976): 1–34; Rossabi, "A Translation of Ch'en Ch'eng's *Hsi-yü fan-kuo chih*," *Ming Studies* 17 (1983): 49–59; Rossabi, "The Tea and Horse Trade with Inner Asia during the Ming," *Journal of Asian History* 4 (1970): 136–68; Rossabi, "Ming China and Turfan, 1406–1517," *Central Asiatic Journal* 16 (1972): 206–25; Rossabi, "Muslim and Central Asian Revolts," in *From Ming to Ch'ing: Conquest, Region, and Continuity in Seventeenth-Century China*, ed. Jonathan D. Spence and John E. Wills, Jr. (New Haven: Yale University Press, 1979), 170–99; Rossabi, "The 'Decline' of the Central Asian Caravan Trade," in *The Rise of Merchant Empires: Long-distance Trade in the Early Modern World, 1350–1750*, ed. James D. Tracy (Cambridge: Cambridge University Press, 1990), 351–70; Goodrich and Fang, eds., *Dictionary*, biography of Ch'en Ch'eng.

10. Goodrich and Fang, eds., *Dictionary*, biographies of Toγon Temür, Toγus Temür, Ayuširidara, Lan Yu, Esen, Altan-qaγan; Waldron, *Great Wall*, 72–164; Frederick W. Mote, "The T'u-mu Incident of 1449," in *Chinese Ways in Warfare*, ed. Frank A. Kierman, Jr., and John K. Fairbank (Cambridge, Mass.: Harvard University Press, 1974), 243–72; Thomas J. Barfield, *The Perilous Frontier: Nomadic Empires and China, 221 BC to AD 1757* (Cambridge, Mass.: Blackwell Publishers, 1989), 229–49; Morris Rossabi, "The Ming and Inner Asia," *Cambridge History of China*, Twitchett and Mote, eds., 221–71; Henry Serruys, "Chinese in Southern Mongolia during the Sixteenth Century," *Monumenta Serica* 18 (1959): 1–95.

11. Barfield, *Perilous Frontier*, 235; David Spindler, "A Twice-Scorned Mongol Woman, the Raid of 1576, and the Building of the Brick Great Wall," *Ming Studies* 60 (2009): 66–94.

12. Goodrich and Fang, eds., *Dictionary*, biographies of Naγaču and Isiha; Rossabi, "Two Ming Envoys"; Henry Serruys, *Sino-Jürčed Relations during the Yung-lo Period*

(1403–1424) (Wiesbaden: Otto Harrassowitz, 1955); Yang Chang et al., *Mingdai Nuergan dusi ji qi weisuo yanjiu* (Henan: Zhongzhou shuhuashe, 1982).

13. Donald N. Clark, "Sino-Korean Tributary Relations under the Ming," *The Cambridge History of China*, ed. Twitchett and Mote, 272–300; James B. Palais, *Confucian Statecraft and Korean Institutions: Yu Hyŏnggwŏn and the Late Chosŏn Dynasty* (Seattle: University of Washington Press, 1996); Kenneth M. Swope, *A Dragon's Head and a Serpent's Tail: Ming China and the First Great East Asian War, 1592–1598* (Norman: University of Oklahoma Press, 2009).

14. Yi-t'ung Wang, *Official Relations between China and Japan: 1368–1549* (Cambridge, Mass.: Harvard University Press, 1953); Jurgis Elisonas, "The Inseparable Trinity: Japan's Relations with China and Korea," in *The Cambridge History of Japan*, vol. 4, ed. John Whitney Hall (Cambridge: Cambridge University Press, 1991), 235–300; Swope, *A Dragon's Head*, 220–21. On piracy, see Charles O. Hucker, "Hu Tsung-hsien's Campaign Against Hsü Hai, 1556," in *Chinese Ways in Warfare*, ed. Kierman and Fairbank, 273–307; Roland L. Higgins, "Pirates in Caps and Gowns: Gentry Law-breaking in the Mid-Ming," *Ming Studies* 10 (1980): 30–37; Kwan-wai So, *Japanese Piracy in Ming China during the 16th Century* (East Lansing: Michigan State University Press, 1975); Goodrich and Fang, eds., *Dictionary*, biographies of Ch'i Chi-kuang, Yü Ta-you, Hu Tsung-hsien; John E. Wills, Jr., "Maritime China from Wang Chih to Shih Lang: Themes in Peripheral History," in *From Ming to Ch'ing*, ed. Spence and Wills, 201–38.

15. Edward L. Dreyer, *Zheng He: China and the Oceans in the Early Ming Dynasty* (New York: Pearson, Longman, 2006); J. V. G. Mills, *Ma Huan: Ying-yai Sheng-lan: The Overall Survey of the Ocean's Shores [1433]* (Cambridge: Published for the Hakluyt Society, at the University Press, 1970); Lo Jung-pang, "The Termination of the Early Ming Naval Expeditions," in *Papers in Honor of Professor Woodbridge Bingham*, ed. James B. Parsons (San Francisco: Chinese Materials Center, 1976), 127–40; Wang Gungwu, "Merchants without Empire: The Hokkien Sojourning Communities," in *The Rise of Merchant Empires*, ed. Tracy, 400–21; Richard Von Glahn, *Fountain of Fortune: Money and Monetary Policy in China, 1000–1700* (Berkeley: University of California Press, 1996), 140; C. R. Boxer, *The Great Ship from Amacon: Annals of Macao and the Old Japan Trade, 1555–1640* (Lisboa: Centro de Estudos Históricos Ultramarinos, 1959); Michael Dillon, "Jingdezhen as a Ming Industrial Center," *Ming Studies* 6 (Spring 1978): 37–44. The literature on the Jesuits and their activities in late Ming China is enormous; a good recent survey is Liam Matthew Brockey, *Journey to the East: The Jesuit Mission to China, 1579–1724* (Cambridge, Mass.: Harvard University Press, 2007).

Chapter 2: Emperors

1. L. Carrington Goodrich and Chaoying Fang, eds., *Dictionary of Ming Biography* (New York: Columbia University Press, 2 vols., 1976), biographies of Chu Yüanchang, Kuo Tzu-hsing, and Empress Ma; Richard Von Glahn, "Ming Taizu *ex nihilo?*"

Ming Studies 55 (2009): 113–41; chapters by Frederick W. Mote, Edward L. Dreyer, and John D. Langlois, Jr., in The Cambridge History of China, Volume 7, Part 1, The Ming Dynasty, 1368–1644, ed. Frederick W. Mote and Denis Twitchett (Cambridge: Cambridge University Press, 1988), 11–181; Edward L. Farmer, Zhu Yuanzhang and Early Ming Legislation: The Reordering of Chinese Society Following the Era of Mongol Rule (Leiden: Brill, 1995); Edward L. Dreyer, Early Ming China: A Political History, 1355–1435 (Stanford: Stanford University Press, 1982); John W. Dardess, Confucianism and Autocracy: Professional Elites in the Founding of the Ming Dynasty (Berkeley: University of California Press, 1983); Sarah Schneewind, A Tale of Two Melons: Emperor and Subject in Ming China (Indianapolis: Hackett Publishing, 2006); Sarah Schneewind, ed., Long Live the Emperor! Uses of the Ming Founder Across Six Centuries of East Asian History (Minneapolis: Society for Ming Studies, 2008); Sarah Schneewind, "Visions and Revisions: Village Policies of the Ming Founder in Seven Phases," T'oung Pao 87 (2001): 319–59.

2. Hok-lam Chan, "The Chien-wen, Yung-lo, Hung-hsi, and Hsüan-te Reigns, 1399–1435," Cambridge History, ed. Mote and Twitchett, 182–304; Goodrich and Fang, eds., Dictionary, biographies of Chu Piao, Chu Yunwen, Chu Ti; Henry Shih-shan Tsai, Perpetual Happiness: The Ming Emperor Yongle (Seattle: University of Washington Press, 2001); David Chan, The Usurpation of the Prince of Yen (San Francisco: Chinese Materials Center, 1975).

3. Goodrich and Fang, eds., Dictionary, biography of Chu Kao-chih.

4. Goodrich and Fang, eds., Dictionary, biography of Chu Chan-chi.

5. Goodrich and Fang, eds., Dictionary, biographies of Chu Ch'i-chen, Wang Chen, and Yü Ch'ien; Cui Xian, Huan ci (Siku quanshu zhenben, 6th series), 6.24b–25a; Yang Shouchen, Yang Wenyi ji (Siming congshu, 7th series), 1.15b–16b.

6. Goodrich and Fang, eds., Dictionary, biography of Chu Ch'i-yü; Ph. De Heer, The Care-taker Emperor: Aspects of the Imperial Institution in Fifteenth-Century China as Reflected in the Political History of the Reign of Chu Ch'i-yü (Leiden: E. J. Brill, 1986).

7. Denis Twitchett and Tilemann Grimm, "The Cheng-t'ung, Ching-t'ai, and T'ien-shun Reigns, 1436–1464," in Cambridge History, ed. Mote and Twitchett, 305–42; John W. Dardess, "Protesting to the Death: The Fuque in Ming Political History," Ming Studies 47 (Spring 2003): 86–125.

8. Goodrich and Fang, eds., Dictionary, biography of Chu Chien-shen; Frederick W. Mote, "The Ch'eng-hua and Hung-chih Reigns, 1465–1505," in Cambridge History, ed. Mote and Twitchett, 343-402.

9. Goodrich and Fang, eds., Dictionary, biography of Chu Yu-t'ang.

10. Goodrich and Fang, eds., Dictionary, biographies of Chu Hou-chao, Chiang Pin, and Liu Chin; James Geiss, "The Cheng-te Reign, 1506–21," in Cambridge History, ed. Mote and Twitchett, 403–39; James Geiss, "The Leopard Quarter during the Cheng-te Reign," Ming Studies 24 (1987): 1–38.

11. Goodrich and Fang, eds., Dictionary, biographies of Chu Hou-ts'ung, T'ao Chung-wen, Yang T'ing-ho, Hsia Yen, Yen Sung; James Geiss, "The Chia-ching Reign, 1522–1566," in Cambridge History, ed. Mote and Twitchett, 440–510; Carney

Fisher, *The Chosen One: Succession and Adoption in the Court of Ming Shizong* (Sydney: Allen and Unwin, 1990); Hung-lam Chu, "The Jiajing Emperor's Interaction with his Lecturers," in *Culture, Courtiers, and Competition: The Ming Court, 1368–1644*, ed. David M. Robinson (Cambridge, Mass.: Harvard University Press, 2008), 186–230; Maggie C. K. Wan, "Building an Immortal Land: the Ming Jiajing Emperor's West Park," *Asia Major* 22, no. 2 (2009): 65–100.

12. Goodrich and Fang, eds., *Dictionary*, biography of Chu Tsai-hou; Ray Huang, "The Lung-ch'ing and Wan-li Reigns, 1567–1620," in *Cambridge History*, ed. Mote and Twitchett, 511–84.

13. Goodrich and Fang, eds., *Dictionary*, biographies of Chu I-chün and Chang Chü-cheng; Yang Shi and Yue Nan, *Kaogu Zhongguo: Dingling dixia xuangongdong yanjiu* (Hainan chubanshe, 2006), 186.

14. Arthur W. Hummel, ed., *Eminent Chinese of the Ch'ing Period* (Washington: United States Government Printing Office, 1943–1944), biography of Chu Chang-lo; William Atwell, "The T'ai-ch'ang, T'ien-ch'i, and Ch'ung-chen Reigns," in *Cambridge History*, ed. Mote and Twitchett, 585–640.

15. John W. Dardess, *Blood and History in China: The Donglin Faction and Its Repression, 1620–1627* (Honolulu: University of Hawaii Press, 2002).

Chapter 3: Governance

1. Romeyn Taylor, "Ming T'ai-tsu and the Nobility of Merit," *Ming Studies* 2 (Spring 1976): 57–69; Thomas Massey, "The Lan Yu Case and Early Ming Military and Society as Revealed in the *Yuzhi nichen lu* (Imperial Record of Rebellious Ministers) of 1393," *Ming Studies* 40 (Fall 1998): 50–71.

2. Shih-shan Henry Tsai, *The Eunuchs in the Ming Dynasty* (Albany: State University of New York Press, 1996).

3. Lynn Struve, book review of Elman's *A Cultural History of Civil Examinations*, in *Ming Studies* 44 (Fall 2000): 116; Benjamin A. Elman, *A Cultural History of Civil Examinations in Late Imperial China* (Berkeley: University of California Press, 2000), 141, 652; Sarah Schneewind, *Community Schools and the State in Ming China* (Stanford: Stanford University Press, 2006); James B. Parsons, "The Ming Dynasty Bureaucracy: Aspects of Background Forces," in *Chinese Government in Ming Times: Seven Studies*, ed. Charles O. Hucker (New York: Columbia University Press, 1969), 175–231; Yan Song, *Qianshantang ji* (Siku quanshu cunmu congshu, 4th ser.), 56.237–38; Zhang Ning, *Fangzhou ji* (Siku quanshu zhenben, 3rd ser.), 309.26.20a–24b; Ni Yue, *Qingqi man'gao* (Wulin wangzhe yizhu), 20.1a–2b.

4. Charles O. Hucker, "Ming Government," in *The Cambridge History of China: Volume 8, the Ming Dynasty, 1368–1644, Part 2*, ed. Denis Twitchett and Frederick W. Mote (Cambridge: Cambridge University Press, 1998), 9–105; Charles O. Hucker, *The Ming Dynasty: Its Origins and Evolving Institutions* (Ann Arbor: Center for Chinese Studies, The University of Michigan, 1978); Charles O. Hucker, *The Censorial System of Ming China* (Stanford: Stanford University Press, 1966).

5. Thomas G. Nimick, *Local Administration in Ming China: The Changing Roles of Magistrates, Prefects, and Provincial Officials* (Minneapolis: Society for Ming Studies, 2008); Ray Huang, *Taxation and Governmental Finance in Sixteenth-Century Ming China* (Cambridge: Cambridge University Press, 1974).

6. *Dictionary of Ming Biography*, ed. L. C. Goodrich and Chaoying Fang (New York: Columbia University Press, 1976), biography of Ch'iu Chün; Hung-lam Chu, "Ch'iu Chün's Ta-hsueh yen-i pu and its Influence in the Sixteenth and Seventeenth Centuries," *Ming Studies* 22 (Fall 1986): 1–32.

7. *Huang Ming jingshi wenbian* (reprint, Taipei: Guolian tushu chuban youxian gongsi, 30 vols., 1964), 22:97–218; Bodo Wiethoff, *Die Chinesische Seeverbotspolitik und der private Überseehandel von 1368 bis 1567* (Hamburg, 1963); Goodrich and Fang, eds., *Dictionary*, biographies of T'u Tse-min and Lin Tao-ch'ien.

8. Otto B. Van der Sprenkel, "High Officials of the Ming: A Note on the Ch'i-ch'ing nien-piao of the Ming History," *Bulletin of the School of Oriental and African Studies* 14 (1962): 87–114; James B. Parsons, "The Ming Dynasty Bureaucracy: Aspects of Background Forces," in *Chinese Government in Ming Times: Seven Studies*, ed. Charles O. Hucker (New York: Columbia University Press, 1969), 177–78.

9. *Guochao xianzheng lu*, ed. Jiao Hong (reprint, Taipei: Taiwan xuesheng shuju, 8 vols., 1965), 7:4544–49.

10. *Guochao xianzheng lu*, 2:1066–70; *Huang Ming jingshi wenbian*, 23:305 ff.; Jie Zhao, "A Decade of Considerable Significance: Late-Ming Factionalism in the Making, 1583–1593," *T'oung Pao* 88 (2002): 143–45; Goodrich and Fang, eds., *Dictionary*, biographies of Chen-k'o, Li Ts'ai, and Lu Nan; Naka Sumio, "Yun Geun-su and Lu Guangzu: Arguments between Chinese and Korean Intellectuals in the Zhu-Lu Disputations," *Tōyōshi kenkyū* 67, no. 3 (2008): 102–40.

11. *Guochao xianzheng lu*, 5:2844–45; *Ming shi*, ed. Zhang Tingyu, ch. 206 (biography of Ma Lu); Gu Yingtai, *Mingshi jishi benmo*, ch. 56 (the Li Fuda case).

Chapter 4: Literati

1. John W. Dardess, "Civil Society in Early Ming China," in *État, Société Civile et Sphère Publique en Asie de l'Est*, ed. Charles Le Blanc and Alain Rocher (Université de Montréal: Sociétés et Cultures de l'Asie, 1998), 37–48; *Dictionary of Ming Biography*, ed. L. C. Goodrich and Fang Chaoying (New York: Columbia University Press, 1976), biographies of Wu Yü-pi, Ch'en Hsien-chang, Hu Chü-jen, Lou Liang, and Wang Shou-jen.

2. John Meskill, "Academies and Politics in the Ming Dynasty," in *Chinese Government in Ming Times: Seven Studies*, ed. Charles O. Hucker (New York: Columbia University Press, 1969), 149–74; John Meskill, *Academies in Ming China: A Historical Essay* (Tucson: University of Arizona Press, 1982); Ronald G. Dimberg, *The Sage and Society: The Life and Thought of Ho Hsin-yin* (Honolulu: The University Press of Hawaii, 1974); Joanna F. Handlin, *Action in Late Ming Thought: The Reorientation of Lü K'un and Other Scholar-Officials* (Berkeley: University of California

Press, 1983); Wm. Theodore de Bary, *The Message of the Mind in Neo-Confucianism* (New York: Columbia University Press, 1989); Wm. Theodore de Bary, *Learning for One's Self: Essays on the Individual in Neo-Confucian Thought* (New York: Columbia University Press, 1991); Goodrich and Fang, eds., *Dictionary*, biographies of Wang Ken, Ho Hsin-yin, Lo Ju-fang, Hsü Chieh; Willard Peterson, "Confucian Learning in Late Ming Thought," in *The Cambridge History of China, Volume 8, The Ming Dynasty, 1368–1644, Part 2*, ed. Denis Twitchett and Frederick W. Mote (Cambridge: Cambridge University Press, 1998), 708–88; Timothy Brook, "Edifying Knowledge: The Building of School Libraries in Ming China," *Late Imperial China* 17, no. 1 (1996): 93–119.

3. Daniel Overmyer, "Boatmen and Buddhas: The Lo-chiao in Ming Dynasty China," *History of Religions* 17 (1978): 284–300; Judith A. Berling, *The Syncretic Religion of Lin Chao-en* (New York: Columbia University Press, 1980); Goodrich and Fang, eds., *Dictionary*, biography of Lin Chao-en.

4. Goodrich and Fang, eds., *Dictionary*, biographies of Li-shih, Fu-teng, Chen-k'o, Chu-hung; Chün-fang Yü, *The Renewal of Buddhism in China: Chu-hung and the Late Ming Synthesis* (New York: Columbia University Press, 1981); Timothy Brook, *Praying for Power: Buddhism and the Formation of Gentry Society in Late-Ming China* (Cambridge, Mass.: Harvard University Press, 1993).

5. *Guochao xianzheng lu*, ed. Jiao Hong (Taipei: Taiwan xuesheng shuju, 1965), 6.3451–52.

6. Goodrich and Fang, eds., *Dictionary*, biography of Yuan Huang; Pei-yi Wu, "Self-Examination and the Confession of Sins in Traditional China," *Harvard Journal of Asiatic Studies* 39 (1979): 5–38; Cynthia J. Brokaw, *The Ledgers of Merit and Demerit: Social Change and Moral Order in Late Imperial China* (Princeton: Princeton University Press, 1991); Kai-wing Chow, "Writing for Success: Printing, Examinations, and Intellectual Change in Late Ming China," *Late Imperial China* 17 (June 1996): 12–57; Kai-wing Chow, *Publishing, Culture, and Power in Early Modern China* (Stanford: Stanford University Press, 2004).

7. Goodrich and Fang, eds., *Dictionary*, biographies of Li Chih and Keng Ting-hsiang; Jin Jiang, "Heresy and Persecution in Late Ming Society: Reinterpreting the Case of Li Zhi," *Late Imperial China* 22, no. 2 (2001): 1–34; William T. Rowe, *Crimson Rain: Seven Centuries of Violence in a Chinese County* (Stanford: Stanford University Press, 2007), 83–108.

8. John W. Dardess, *Blood and History in China: The Donglin Faction and Its Repression, 1620–1627* (Honolulu: University of Hawaii Press, 2002), 177, for the quote.

9. Arthur W. Hummel, ed., *Eminent Chinese of the Ch'ing Period* (Washington: United States Government Printing Office, 1943–1944), biography of Chang P'u; William S. Atwell, "From Education to Politics: The Fu She," in *The Unfolding of Neo-Confucianism*, ed. Wm. Theodore de Bary (New York: Columbia University Press, 1975), 333–68; Jerry Dennerline, *The Chia-ting Loyalists: Confucian Leadership and Social Change in Seventeenth-Century China* (New Haven: Yale University Press, 1981), 43–56.

10. Goodrich and Fang, eds., *Dictionary*, biography of Kao Ch'i; F. W. Mote, *The Poet Kao Ch'i, 1336–1374* (Princeton: Princeton University Press, 1962); John W. Dardess, "The Yuan-Ming Transition: Liu Song as Witness" (paper presented at the Traditional China Seminar, Columbia University, New York, New York, Spring 2005).

11. Goodrich and Fang, eds., *Dictionary*, biographies of Li Tung-yang, Li Meng-yang, Hsü Chen-ch'ing, T'ang Yin, Wen Chen-ming, Chu Yun-ming; the quotation is from Zhang Tingyu, ed., *Ming shih*, ch. 285 (introduction to biographies of men of letters).

12. Goodrich and Fang, eds., *Dictionary*, biographies of T'ang Shun-chih, Hsü Wei, Li K'ai-hsien, K'ang Hai, Mao K'un, Kuei Yu-kuang; Katherine Carlitz, "Wang Shizhen and the Myth of Gui Youguang," *Ming Studies* 55 (Spring 2007): 34–74.

13. Goodrich and Fang, eds., *Dictionary*, biographies of Wang Shih-chen, Wang Tao-chen, Wang Tao-k'un, Yang Chi-sheng, Wang Hsi-chüeh; Sun Weiguo, "Different Types of Scholar-Official in 16th-Century China: The Interlaced Careers of Wang Shizhen and Zhang Juzheng," *Ming Studies* 53 (Spring 2006): 4–50; Kenneth J. Hammond, "Wang Shizhen as Partisan: The Case of Yang Jisheng," *Ming Studies* 53 (Spring 2006): 51–71; Peter K. Bol, "Looking to Wang Shizhen: Hu Yinglin (1551–1602) and Late-Ming Alternatives to Neo-Confucian Learning," *Ming Studies* 53 (Spring 2006): 99–137; Alison Hardie, "'Massive Structure' or 'Spacious Naturalness'? Aesthetic Choices in the Wang Families' Gardens in Taicang," *Ming Studies* 55 (Spring 2007): 3–33; Kenneth J. Hammond, *Pepper Mountain: The Life, Death and Posthumous Career of Yang Jisheng* (London: Routledge, 2007). The first quotation is from Wang Xijue's epitaph for Wang Shizhen, in *Guochao xianzheng lu*, ed. Jiao Hong, 3.1896. The second quotation is from Bol, "Looking to Wang Shizhen," 102.

14. Goodrich and Fang, eds., *Dictionary*, biographies of Chung Hsing, T'an Yüan-chen, Yüan Hung-tao; Chih-p'ing Chou, *Yüan Hung-tao and the Kung-an School* (Cambridge: Cambridge University Press, 1988).

15. Wai-yee Li, "The Collector, the Connoisseur, and Late-Ming Sensibility," *T'oung Pao* 81 (1995): 269–302; Craig Clunas, *Superfluous Things: Material Culture and Social Status in Early Modern China* (Urbana: University of Illinois Press, 1991); Craig Clunas, *Fruitful Sites: Garden Culture in Ming Dynasty China* (Durham: Duke University Press, 1996); Joanna Handlin Smith, *The Art of Doing Good: Charity in Late Ming China* (Berkeley: University of California Press, 2009); Willard Peterson, "Confucian Learning in Late Ming Thought," in *Cambridge History*, ed. Twitchett and Mote, 708–88; Timothy Brook, *The Confusions of Pleasure: Commerce and Culture in Ming China* (Berkeley: University of California Press, 1998); John Meskill, *Gentlemanly Interests and Wealth on the Yangtze Delta* (Ann Arbor: Association for Asian Studies, 1994); Jonathan D. Spence, *Return to Dragon Mountain: Memories of a Late Ming Man* (New York: Viking, 2007); Jaret Wayne Weisfogel, *A Late Ming Vision for Local Community: Ritual, Law, and Social Ferment in the Proposals of Guan Zhidao*, ed. Sarah Schneewind (Minneapolis: Society for Ming Studies, 2010).

Chapter 5: Outlaws

1. Zhao Yi, *Nianerh shi zhaji* (2 vols., Taipei: Shijie shuju, 1958), 2:487.

2. Gu Yingtai, *Mingshi jishi benmo*, ch. 57 (The Datong mutiny).

3. *Dictionary of Ming Biography*, ed. L. C. Goodrich and Fang Chaoying (New York: Columbia University Press, 1976), biography of T'ang Sai-erh; Gu Yingtai, ch. 23 (Pacification of the Shandong rebels).

4. Goodrich and Fang, eds., *Dictionary*, biography of Hsü Hung-ju; Gu Yingtai, ch. 70 (Pacification of Xu Hongru).

5. Gu Yingtai, ch. 31 (Pacification of the Zhejiang and Fujian Bandits); Goodrich and Fang, eds., *Dictionary*, biographies of Teng Mao-ch'i and Yeh Tsung-liu.

6. Gu Yingtai, ch. 38 (Pacification of the Yunyang Bandits); Goodrich and Fang, eds., *Dictionary*, biography of Hsiang Chung.

7. Gu Yingtai, ch. 46 (Pacification of the Sichuan Bandits).

8. James W. Tong, *Disorder under Heaven: Collective Violence in the Ming Dynasty* (Stanford: Stanford University Press, 1991).

9. Gu Yingtai, chs. 47 (The Chenhao Revolt) and 48 (Pacification of the Nan'gan Bandits); John E. Herman, *Amid the Clouds and Mist: China's Colonization of Guizhou, 1200–1700* (Cambridge, Mass.: Harvard University Press, 2007), 129; Larry Israel, "To Accommodate or Subjugate: Wang Yangming's Settlement of Conflict in Guangxi in Light of Ming Political and Strategic Culture," *Ming Studies* 60 (2009): 4–44; Gao Dai, *Hongyou lu*, 1235–38.

10. Gu Yingtai, *Mingshi jishi benmo*, ch. 45 (Pacification of the Hebei Bandits); Gao Dai, *Hongyou lu*, 1238–54; David M. Robinson, *Bandits, Eunuchs, and the Son of Heaven: Rebellion and the Economy of Violence in Mid-Ming China* (Honolulu: University of Hawaii Press, 2001); Roger V. Des Forges, *Cultural Centrality and Political Change in Chinese History: Northeast Henan in the Fall of the Ming* (Stanford: Stanford University Press, 2003), 169–73.

11. Liu Yi'nan, *Li Zicheng jinian fukao* (Beijing, 1983), 3–4.

12. For Li's death, cf. Liu Yi'nan, *Li Zicheng*, 303.

13. Zhang Tingyu, ed., *Ming shi*, ch. 260 (biography of Yang He); Chen-main Wang, *The Life and Career of Hung Ch'eng-ch'ou (1593–1665): Public Service in a Time of Dynastic Change* (Ann Arbor: Association for Asian Studies, 1999), 37–48.

14. Wang, *The Life and Career*, 49–57.

15. Zhang Tingyu, ed., *Ming shi*, ch. 261 (biography of Lu Xiangsheng).

16. Goodrich and Fang, eds., *Dictionary*, biographies of Hsiung Wen-ts'an and Yang Ssu-ch'ang; Lo Jung-pang, "Policy Formulation and Decision-Making on Issues Respecting Peace and War," in *Chinese Government in Ming Times: Seven Studies* (New York: Columbia University Press, 1969), 68–69.

17. Liu Yi'nan, *Li Zicheng*, 4.

18. Li Wenzhih, *Wan Ming minbian* (Hong Kong: Yuandong tushu gongsi, 1966), 72–73.

19. Li Wenzhi, *Wan Ming*, 73–88; William T. Rowe, *Crimson Rain: Seven Centuries of Violence in a Chinese County* (Stanford: Stanford University Press, 2007), 140–42.

20. James B. Parsons, *Peasant Rebellions of the Late Ming Dynasty* (Tucson: University of Arizona Press, 1970), 175.

21. Arthur W. Hummel, ed., *Eminent Chinese of the Ch'ing Period* (Washington: United States Government Printing Office, 1943–1944), biographies of Sun K'e-wang and Li Ting-kuo; Parsons, *Peasant Rebellions*, 181.

22. For the *hao han* tradition, see W. J. F. Jenner, *The Tyranny of History: The Roots of China's Crisis* (London: Allan Lane, The Penguin Press, 1992), 203–5.

23. Parsons, *Peasant Rebellions*, 19–20.

24. For Li Zicheng's story, I have mainly had recourse to Parsons, *Peasant Rebellions*, 90–166; Des Forges, *Cultural Centrality*, 204–311; Li Wenzhi, *Wan Ming*, 97–195; and Frederic Wakeman, "The Shun Interregnum of 1644," in *From Ming to Ch'ing*, ed. Jonathan D. Spence and John E. Wills, Jr., 39–88.

~

Further Reading

Anyone with a serious interest in exploring the entirety of Ming history should be aware of three important English-language resources. One is the *Dictionary of Ming Biography*, published in two volumes by Columbia University Press in 1976, and cited often in the endnotes. It is a treasure trove of the lives of a very wide range of people—emperors and empresses, princes, officials, military men, eunuchs, Confucian activists and thinkers, Buddhist priests, Daoist adepts, Jesuits, poets, novelists, playwrights, artists, experts of various sorts, pirates and bandits, plus a smattering of other men and women of the time. A second is the *Cambridge History of China: The Ming Dynasty 1368–1644*, also in two volumes, and also cited many times in the notes. The first volume, published in 1988, is a well-written chronological history, with chapters by different authors centered upon each of the emperors. The second volume, published ten years later, consists of fifteen chapters devoted to special topics, art and literature excepted. The third resource is the journal *Ming Studies*, published twice yearly since 1975.

Several other comprehensive accounts of the Ming written in English should be noted. One is Albert Chan's *The Glory and Fall of the Ming Dynasty*, published by the University of Oklahoma Press in 1982. Chan divides the Ming into rising and declining phases; thirteen chapters take up, in well-documented detail, government, army, culture, ethics, religion, and economics—or, rather, the fiscal system—during each phase. F. W. Mote's *Imperial China: 900–1800* (Cambridge: Harvard University Press, 1999) devotes ten of its thirty-six chapters to the Ming. These chapters occupy some three hundred pages and almost form a book in themselves. Timothy Brook's *The Troubled Empire: China in the Yuan and Ming Dynasties* (Cambridge: Harvard University Press, 2010) consists of ten chapters covering such topics as climate change and ecology, family and society, foreign trade, consumption, administrative geography, aspects of high politics, and much else. The same author's *The Confusions of Pleasure: Commerce and Culture in Ming China* (Berkeley: University of California Press, 1996) also covers the entire Ming in the context of shifting elite attitudes toward frugality and luxury. My own *A Ming Society: T'ai-ho County, Kiangsi, in the Fourteenth to Seventeenth Centuries* (Berkeley: University of California Press, 1996) also covers the whole Ming era from the point of view of local society, bringing in such themes as land use, demographic change, family and lineage, official recruitment, and the impact of philosophical movements.

Some good recent books focus on individual aspects of Ming history, but are not cited in the endnotes. Michael Marme's *Suzhou: Where the Goods of all the Provinces Converge* (Stanford: Stanford University Press, 2005) places Suzhou city and its elites in a context of urban and commercial growth. Harry Miller's *State versus Gentry in Late Ming Dynasty China: 1572–1644* (New York: Palgrave Macmillan, 2009) traces six phases in seventy years of Beijing factional struggle. Jiang Yonglin's *The Mandate of Heaven and the Great Ming Code* (Seattle: University of Washington Press, 2011) analyzes the cosmological scaffolding of Ming law as it pertained to state religion, foreign and intra-ethnic affairs, and official malfeasance. And Sarah Schneewind's *A Tale of Two Melons: Emperor and Subject in Ming China* (Indianapolis: Hackett Publishing, 2006) is a detailed exploration of the complex ramifications of a seemingly simple gesture, the presentation by a local peasant of a felicitous anomaly, two melons sharing one stalk, to the Ming founder Taizu in 1372. Her account shows how and why, over the long term, the affair prompted a struggle, involving the imperial center and the locale of origin, over how to interpret the anomaly, with local people and their interests quite able to hold their own.

So rich and extensive are the Ming sources that all this English-language publication barely scratches the surface of what might be written and debated and discussed about this era, which spans Europe's late medieval and early modern phases. One looks forward to the books and articles and other studies that will surely be forthcoming about Ming China in future years.

Index

~

About the Author

John W. Dardess received his Ph.D. from Columbia University in 1968. Since 2002, he has been Professor Emeritus of History, University of Kansas. He is the author of four books that deal with Yuan and Ming China. His latest book is *Governing China, 150–1850* (Indianapolis: Hackett Publishing, 2010).